Pfalz Aces
of World War 1

SERIES EDITOR: TONY HOLMES

OSPREY AIRCRAFT OF THE ACES • 71

Pfalz Aces
of World War 1

Greg VanWyngarden

OSPREY
PUBLISHING

Front Cover
On 23 March 1918, Bavarian *Jagdstaffel* 34b was in the thick of the aerial combat that accompanied Germany's last great gamble on the Western Front. Just 48 hours earlier, the great Amiens Offensive, generally known as *Kaiserschlacht*, had erupted and the German storm troops had made great gains. One of the *Jasta* 34b pilots aloft that day was Ltn d R Rudolf Stark, who had arrived at the unit only a month earlier, and had yet to attain his first victory. Stark was flying Pfalz D III 4064/17, marked with his lilac band. In his book *Die Jagdstaffel unsere Heimat,* Stark would later recount the day's events;

'We fly forward. Péronne is burning. The smoke of many conflagrations rises up. We find no adversaries in the heights, so we drop down, often as low as 100 metres from the ground. Below us, English artillery is in retreat, khaki infantry hastens westward.

'We fly over Péronne. My engine seizes up and will work only spasmodically. I must turn back. The signal flares I fire pass unnoticed in the smoke. I must go back to the front alone. All around me is the smoke of the burning town and I lose my direction.

'Suddenly two machines jump up before me – English two-seaters. They attack me. I cannot rely on my engine now, but I mean to sell my life as dearly as possible and so attack one of the Englishmen. A couple of shots – guns jammed – yes, they would at such a moment. I feel myself defenceless, and in my rage I try to ram an enemy's machine. One of the Englishmen has lost height in a turn. I bear down on him, my fingers press the trigger-buttons, and suddenly the guns begin to fire again. Then I see the observer in the other machine collapse and his pilot lurch forward. I pull my stick hard and just get past the English machine, which goes down on to its nose and falls vertically. It crashes in an old shell hole amid the ruins of Barleux.

'The other Englishman breaks off the combat and vanishes in the mist. I make an effort to find my way, trying to steer an eastward course by my compass. My engine runs worse and worse, but at last I see the front, with field-grey soldiers below me once more. My petrol is nearly done. Below me is shell-hole country, which is far from suitable for an emergency landing. I carry on. At last a wide field extends before me – an aerodrome. I land on the last drop of petrol and find myself at Villers-le-Sec. That means I have drifted a long way southward. The mechanics of *Jagdstaffel* 79 attend to my machine, and then I start off home.'

Stark's initial victory was recorded as a DH 4, one of three victims claimed by the *Jasta* that day. He would go on to more success, adding a further four victories to his score while flying the elegant silver-grey Pfalz D III and D IIIa with *Staffel* 34b. Stark would subsequently command *Jasta* 35b and finish the war with 11 victories (*Cover artwork by Mark Postlethwaite*)

First published in Great Britain in 2006 by Osprey Publishing
Midland House, West Way, Botley, Oxford, OX2 0PH
443 Park Avenue South, New York, NY, 10016, USA
E-mail; info@ospreypublishing.com

© 2006 Osprey Publishing Limited

ISBN 10: 1-84176-998-3
ISBN 13: 978-1-84176-998-1

Edited by Tony Holmes
Page design by Mark Holt
Cover Artwork by Mark Postlethwaite
Aircraft Profiles by Harry Dempsey
Line Artwork by Mark Styling
Index by Alan Thatcher
Originated by PPS Grasmere, Leeds, UK
Printed and bound in China through Bookbuilders

06 07 08 09 10   10 9 8 7 6 5 4 3 2 1

For a catalogue of all books published by Osprey please contact:

NORTH AMERICA
Osprey Direct, c/o Random House Distribution Center,
400 Hahn Road, Westminster, MD 21157
E-mail:info@ospreydirect.com

ALL OTHER REGIONS
Osprey Direct UK, P.O. Box 140 Wellingborough, Northants, NN8 2FA, UK
E-mail: info@ospreydirect.co.uk
www.ospreypublishing.com

EDITOR'S NOTE
To make this best-selling series as authoritative as possible, the Editor would be interested in hearing from any individual who may have relevant photographs, documentation or first-hand experiences relating to the world's elite pilots, and their aircraft, of the various theatres of war. Any material used will be credited to its original source. Please write to Tony Holmes via e-mail at; tony.holmes@osprey-jets.freeserve.co.uk

CONTENTS

INTRODUCTION

'The Fokker was a bloodstock animal that answered to the slightest movement of the hand and could almost guess the rider's will in advance. The Pfalz was a sluggish work horse which fought the bridle and had to be controlled with a strong halter.'

Thus did the Bavarian ace, and former cavalryman, Rudolf Stark state his opinion of the Pfalz D XII. Although he was comparing the late-war D XII biplane fighter to the superb Fokker D VII, it could be said that a similar attitude was frequently felt toward the other fighter types to emerge from the Pfalz Flugzeugwerke. Attractive and generally competent designs when judged on their own merits, Pfalz aircraft were, however, almost invariably found wanting when compared with better-known contemporary machines.

The first Pfalz fighters were monoplanes based closely on the French Morane-Saulnier type H design – these were considered inferior to the contemporary Fokker Eindeckers. The most widely known and numerous Pfalz aircraft were the sleek, elegant D III and its successor the D IIIa. These fighters were produced in quantity and flown successfully by many German pilots of the *Jagdstaffeln* (fighter units), and they will form the primary subjects of this volume. Even so, the D III was never as widely used or as favoured as the contemporary Albatros fighters.

Quite a few pilots achieved success in the D IIIa but the type failed to achieve a formidable reputation. The last Pfalz designs to see action were the compact rotary-engined D VIII interceptor and the robust but maligned D XII, and both are also featured in this book.

One additional note. In preparing this instalment of the *Osprey Aircraft of the Aces* series, the author has been forced to broaden the definition of what exactly constitutes a 'Pfalz ace'. While German archival information records the victories attained by the *Jasta* pilots, this data rarely gives precise information regarding what type of aircraft the victorious airmen flew. For the first half of 1918, many *Jagdstaffeln* were, by necessity, operating a mix of Albatros, Pfalz or Fokker machines, and it is often difficult, if not impossible, to know which aeroplane a pilot used to gain a particular victory. Many aces known to have flown Pfalz designs most likely obtained the majority of their successes while flying other types.

For the purposes of this book, a 'Pfalz ace' is therefore an ace who is documented as having flown a Pfalz aircraft at one time in his career as a *Jagdflieger*, and not necessarily someone who scored five victories (or indeed any victories) in a Pfalz. In the absence of better information, accounts of and by 'lesser' pilots who also flew Pfalz designs are also covered.

Greg VanWyngarden
St Charles, Iowa
March 2006

PFALZ MONOPLANES

The Pfalz Flugzeugwerke GmbH, located at Speyer on the Rhine, in Bavaria, was founded in 1913 by the three enterprising Eversbusch brothers, Alfred, Ernst and Walter. Initially, the firm intended to obtain licence rights from the Albatros Company of Johannisthal to produce that company's aircraft in Bavaria. When that agreement fell through, the Pfalz firm obtained financing and assistance from Gustav Otto in Munich to build Otto B-type pusher biplanes under licence for the Pfalz flying school. This was done at the urging of the Bavarian Flying Service, as Bavaria was the most independent and powerful of all the states in the Imperial Germany next to Prussia, and maintained its own flying service.

Alfred Eversbusch soon realised that the Otto machines were hardly competitive with current French aircraft, and in February 1914 the firm procured a licence agreement with the French Morane-Saulnier firm to construct its type L and H monoplanes in Bavaria.

In July of that year, Walter Eversbusch gained his pilot's certificate from the Morane-Saulnier school in Paris, and he would serve as his firm's chief test pilot until a fatal crash on 1 June 1916.

While the Pfalz Company is most famous for its streamlined D III and D IIIa fighters of 1917-18, its first aircraft to see combat in World War 1 were rotary-engined monoplanes which were strict copies of Morane-Saulnier designs. Several airmen who would later gain renown as aces gained their initial experience in these machines.

When the Great War erupted in August 1914, the Pfalz company had completed only three parasol monoplanes based on the Morane-Saulnier Type L, three shoulder-wing monoplane copies of the Type H and three Otto biplanes for the Bavarian air service. Eventually, some 60 Type L two-seater parasols – numbered P1 to P60 – would be produced. These would be given the German military designations of Pfalz A I (powered by the 80 hp Oberursel U 0 rotary) and A II (with the 100 hp Oberursel U I). These parasols did yeoman service with Bavarian reconnaissance units in the first year of the war, and they would later serve as trainers.

One pilot who would gain a wealth of experience on the Pfalz monoplanes was 22-year-old Max Holtzem, a pre-war aviator who had joined the 3rd *Flieger Bataillon* at Köln on 14 October 1913. Though he would never become an ace by official standards, Holtzem enjoyed a lengthy and varied flying career that lasted the entirety of World War 1, and his story is inextricably tied to the Pfalz firm and its aircraft.

After wartime service with *Feld Flieger Abteilungen* 9 and 34, Holtzem was sent to the Pfalz factory on 17 April 1915 for training on parasols and single-seater monoplanes. He lived a long life in aviation and spent his last years in California, where he remembered;

A Pfalz Parasol of *Feldflieger Abteilung* 9b is readied to have its engine run up, with the wheels chocked and two mechanics holding down the tail. The location is Toblach, in the Puster Valley of the Dolomites. The backdrop to this photograph gives a good impression of the rugged terrain these machines had to fly over. The Pfalz monoplane was a licence-built copy of the Morane-Saulnier Type L Parasol. The Pfalz had a much shorter take-off run than the unit's other aircraft, the LVG B I, and was better suited to the Alpine conditions

'I was a very happy guy when I strolled down the road on a beautiful early morning in the spring of 1915 to the Pfalz aircraft factory at Speyer am Rhein, not far from the old cathedral – the *Speyer Dom* – and near the shoreline of the Rhine River. Now I would become a single-seater pilot in these marvelous little aeroplanes, all by myself, and doing what I wanted to do, instead of being a mere chauffeur! My instructor, Walter Eversbusch, was young, and a dreamer just as I was. He had just finished the training of his first pupil, Uffz (Eduard) Böhme. I was shown the intricacies of handling the little ships that had no stabilisers of any kind.'

Holtzem recalled that the Pfalz monoplanes were tricky to fly, and had to be carefully rigged with the control column dead centre. If the column was let loose during flight, the aeroplane would 'do almost anything'. It might roll because the wings would warp, or would dive or climb since the rudder had no fin and there were no horizontal stabilisers, just elevators.

The controls were extremely sensitive, and take-offs and landings were difficult. With the Gnome-type Oberursel engine, there was no way to throttle back – the engine was wide-open or nothing. The pilot had a 'blip' switch on top of the stick that interrupted the ignition but kept the engine clean and running – this is how the pilot reduced power. When such an aircraft came in to land one would hear the famous 'brrrp – brrrp', which is why they were called *Schurpsen* by the Germans.

When queried about the reliability of the frail-looking Pfalz A I Parasols, Holtzem replied, 'I am often asked about the structural strength of these early aeroplanes. They were so light and looked so flimsy. They stood up surprisingly well to rough and most demanding service.' When Walter Eversbusch was killed on Pentecost Day of 1916, Holtzem took over as chief Pfalz test pilot.

Although constructed in small numbers, the Pfalz A I played a key role in the first great exploit of the eventual 'Blue Max' winner Otto Kissenberth. This 19-victory ace was born in Landshut, Niederbayern (Lower Bavaria) on 26 February 1893. An avid mountaineer, he gained a mechanical engineering degree at the technical college in Munich after studying French language and literature at the University of Grenoble. After completing his engineering curriculum, Kissenberth passed his flying examinations at the Otto Works in Munich.

When war broke out, he volunteered for duty at FEA I in Schleissheim and finished his training at the Johannisthal School near Berlin. Kissenberth reported to F. Fl. Abt. 8b ('b' for Bavarian) on 21 January 1915, and received his Pilot's Badge the same day. He sustained a severe hip wound in aerial combat over the Vosges Mountains on 21 March, but returned to the front two months later. In July Kissenberth was assigned to F. Fl. Abt. 9b, which was ordered to perform the duties of *Alpenkorps Flieger Abt* (Alpine Corps aviation unit) for the Bavarian army in the Dolomites, or Tyrolean Alps.

On 23 May 1915, Italy had declared war on Germany's ally Austria-Hungary, but not on Germany. This left Austria's southern flank in the Alps almost completely unprotected. The campaign against Austria-Hungary's primary Russian enemy in the east was in full swing, absorbing most of the Dual Monarchy's military resources. For the defence of a mountainous border with Italy, stretching 350 kilometres, Austria had only a volunteer territorial rifle corps, thus it had to retreat northward. Kaiser Wilhelm came to the aid of his ally, and on 25 May 1915 initial elements of the partially complete German *Alpenkorps* arrived in Tyrol.

The newly formed F. Fl. Abt. 9b was ordered from Schleissheim to Tyrol on 1 June. Its commander was the distinguished pre-war pilot Oblt Franz Hailer. Following a taxing search for suitable airfields, the unit settled in at the parade ground south of Brixen, equipped with LVG B I biplanes and Pfalz Parasols. The difficult terrain and weather conditions caused many complications. Compounding these difficulties were strict orders from the Kaiser that German troops (and aircraft) were not to cross the Italian border in order to avoid war with Italy. The unit soon transferred to Toblach in the Puster Valley. It was from that mountain meadow aerodrome that Kissenberth and others would take off on a daring – and somewhat clandestine – mission.

A bombing raid was to be made on Italian troops and supply depots at Cortina d'Ampezzo, which was actually then in Austrian territory, but occupied by the Italians (thus, they would not technically be flying into Italy). Each of the Parasols was furnished with makeshift bomb racks for five 4.5-kg Carbonit bombs on each side of the fuselage. In order to allow the heavily-loaded monoplanes to climb over the Alps, they would be flown without observers. On 3 June Kissenberth's *Abteilung* was ordered to paint large red and white stripes on the fuselage and the wing undersides of the Parasols. The red/white markings were part of the national insignia of the Austro-Hungarian *Luftfahrtruppe*, thus this ruse was designed to give the Italians the impression that the Parasols were Austrian.

After several delays, the raid was ultimately scheduled for the late afternoon of 31 July. The weather cleared somewhat, but a high cloud cover and squall-like winds remained as the three Pfalz were prepared for take-off. Vfw Kissenberth in Parasol P39 struggled off the airfield first, followed by Uffz Eduard Böhme then Ltn Ferdinand März. After climbing to 300 metres the third Parasol was caught in a violent downward squall and März crashed fatally. This went unnoticed by the first two pilots, and they continued on their way. Kissenberth would later write;

'I soon lost sight of my comrades. First of all, I tried to gain as much height as rapidly as possible. After nearly half an hour I was ready. I left the Puster Valley behind, flew by Dürrenstein Mountain, which always provided the pilot with particularly strong gusts, crept past the

The future *Pour le Mérite* ace Otto Kissenberth demonstrated how he hoped to operate a camera that had been especially fitted to his Pfalz Parasol P39 in the hope of capturing the results of his bombing raid on Cortina. Note the 'P39' painted on the underside of the centre section behind his head, and the translucent quality of the clear-doped fabric. Kissenberth wrote, 'I also installed my camera, although I could read on the faces of the observers that they would never believe one of the pilots capable of taking decent photographs'. As it turned out, by the time the Parasols dropped their bombs it was too dark for photos anyway

An evocative scene of bustling activity at Toblach field shows the newly painted Parasols of F. Fl. Abt. 9b being prepared for their mission to Cortina on 31 July 1915. The red and white markings on the fuselage and wing were a bit of subterfuge meant to disguise the Pfalz as Austro-Hungarian machines. The box attached to the side of the fuselage beneath the cockpit was an improvised bomb-dropping device. Four Parasols painted in the special markings are seen, although only three pilots were detailed for the mission

powerfully formed rock walls of the Croda Rossa and inside the tall peaks surrounding the Cortina basin – Monte Pelmo, Tofana, Cristallo, Sorapiss – all names which touched a mountain climber's heart. But that day their natural beauty was not much inspiration to me. Much more valuable was the discovery that Cima Pomagagnon was covered up with a cloud bank, and I was therefore able to fly over undisturbed. The Italians, who had yesterday nastily inflicted many hits on my new Parasol from there with their machine guns, were surely enraged that they today could not do any harm to the *aviatico maledetto* ("damned Aviatik").

'Meanwhile, the first houses of Cortina were already in sight. I was at 1500 metres over them, prepared everything ready for the drop, flew precisely over the objective, estimated how long I must hold off and then let the seven bombs drop. I could not observe the hits with certainty because I had my hands full just maintaining control of my machine in the squalls, which were especially violent here. Hastily, I made off. I could not take any photographs of Cortina, as it was already too dark below.

Ltn Ferdinand März (seen in the inset) was killed in this crash as he took off for the Cortina raid on 31 July. The red and white markings are clearly visible on the fuselage sides and undersides of the wing – note that these did not extend to the underside of the fuselage

'I followed the course to Cristallo, because the Pomagagnon lay free of clouds by then and I wanted to avoid the threatening machine guns there. I flew only a few feet over the Cristallo glacier. Looking at its eternal ice in the dark blue crevasses, the beauty and enchantment of the flight over the high mountain range came to me with conviction. The last rays of the sinking sun, refracted by the scraps of mist into rainbow colours, lay on the powerful summits and peaks.

'When I landed I received the sad news that one of my comrades had crashed fatally shortly after the start. Our flight had success, though. A few days afterwards, our leader, Oblt Hailer, informed us that statements from prisoners revealed that 11 bombs had hit their targets.'

The Cortina mission was the zenith of the operational activities of the Pfalz Parasol. On 9 August 1915 F. Fl. Abt. 9b was ordered to the Western Front. The unit soon transferred to Colmar, in Alsace, where it continued operations with the Pfalz A I, along with other machines. It was a different Pfalz aircraft, however, that would play a further role in Kissenberth's career.

PFALZ E-TYPE FIGHTERS

On 18 April 1915 an event occurred which would drastically alter the character of aerial warfare, as well as the future of the Pfalz firm. The French pre-war aviator Roland Garros, then a pilot with *Escadrille* MS 26, was captured when his Morane-Saulnier L (the type that was the basis for the Pfalz A I) was shot down by ground fire near Ingelmunster. Working with Raymond Saulnier, Garros had experimentally fitted a forward-firing Hotchkiss machine gun in front of his cockpit and attached metal bullet deflectors to the propeller blades. With this crude device, Garros had knocked down three German aircraft since 1 April. Naturally, German authorities found his installation fascinating, and were inspired to immediately try something similar on their own machines.

Fortunately for *Idflieg* (the *Inspektion der Fliegertruppen,* or Inspectorate of aviation troops), the brilliant Dutch aircraft designer Anthony Fokker had already been working on a superior mechanical synchronisation system. This permitted a machine gun to fire through the propeller arc with no risk of hitting the propeller, and was no doubt 'inspired' by a similar method patented by LVG chief engineer Franz Schneider in 1913.

Fokker successfully installed his mechanism on one of his own Fokker M5K monoplanes, which were themselves loosely based on Morane-Saulnier designs (but were, in fact, great improvements over the French designs). On 16 May 1915, *Idflieg* invited Pfalz Director Eversbusch to observe firing trials of the Fokker synchronisation system. The Pfalz Company was no doubt involved because the firm was already manufacturing copies of Garros' Morane-Saulnier, which had provided the incentive for the adoption of the system in the first place.

Pfalz engineers began to experiment with arming their own monoplanes with synchronised guns following the demonstration in May. Information on the development of the armed version of the Pfalz monoplane is lacking, but an *Idflieg* contract for 25 E I and ten E II fighters was in place by 28 September 1915.

The E I was powered by the seven-cylinder 80 hp Oberursel U 0 rotary, while the E II utilised the nine-cylinder 100 hp Oberursel U I, and had wings of increased area. Both mounted a single LMG 08 gun, popularly

Kurt Weil recalled that, because of their white fabric and black-outlined surfaces, these early Pfalz aircraft were known as 'flying death announcements'. In this case, the nickname was almost too appropriate. Oblt Rudolf Berthold sustained major injuries when he crashed in this Pfalz E IV from a height of 100 metres only a few minutes after take-off on 25 April 1916. This was the first in a long string of wounds that would plague the future high-scoring ace throughout the war

Even budding aces can have a bad day. The future 'Blue Max' winner Ernst Udet crashed this Pfalz E IV when he was flying as a member of *KEK* Habsheim. Since the rudder is missing, it appears that the aircraft flipped onto its back, and was subsequently set right side up for this photograph. Udet scored no victories in this machine, but would end the war as Germany's ranking surviving ace with 62 victories. The Pfalz E IV was powered by the 160-hp Oberursel U III twin-row rotary, and was equipped with twin Spandau LMG 08 machine guns

known as the 'Spandau'. Four months after the famed Fokker E I arrived at the Front in June 1915, the first examples of the Pfalz E I made their appearance in the combat zone.

The Pfalz Eindeckers, however, would never become as popular as the superior Fokkers. The introduction of the Pfalz E III parasol fighter and even the twin-gunned E IV with a 160 hp Oberursel U III twin-row rotary failed to enhance the reputation of Pfalz products. By the end of April 1916 there were 56 Pfalz monoplane fighters at the Front (27 of them E Is), compared with 173 Fokker E-types. Two months later there were 51 Pfalz fighters recorded (30 E IIs among them) and 137 Fokkers. It was a case of too little, too late, for the Pfalz E-types simply failed to make an impact. From the Allied pilots' point of view, the Pfalz monoplanes were totally unknown, and they were invariably reported as Fokkers due to their similar configuration.

Photographic evidence indicates that several successful Fokker aces and aces-to-be flew Pfalz E-types operationally at least a few times. As with the first Fokkers, the Pfalz were parceled out to assorted reconnaissance squadrons and, occasionally, to early makeshift fighter units known as *Kampfeinsitzer Kommandos* (*KEK*, single-seater fighter commands).

Pilots frequently expressed preference for Fokker designs and their disgust with the Pfalz machines 'because of their insufficient performance'. Furthermore, Fl. Abt. 71 submitted a report in January 1916 that one of its Pfalz fighters had suffered elevator failure. It was eventually revealed that the junction of the elevator tube spar and elevator control was weak and required reinforcement. Due to their unpopularity, many Pfalz E-types were sent to the Eastern Front or other theatres where the opposition was not as intense as in the west – they served in Russia, on the Macedonian/Bulgarian front and even Palestine.

One budding ace who certainly gained experience on Pfalz monoplanes was Otto Kissenberth. Having returned to France with F. Fl. Abt. 9b, he had been promoted to Offizier-Stellvertreter on 27 August 1915, and commissioned on 11 November. After receiving the Iron Cross First Class on 10 January 1916, Kissenberth was one of the pilots selected for the unit's fighter detachment, known as *KEK* Ensisheim – also located at Colmar in the *Armee Abteilung* B sector.

Kissenberth flew both Fokker monoplanes and a variety of Pfalz E-types during his service in the *KEK*, although he failed to score any confirmed victories in these machines. Nonetheless, his aggressive character and determination earned him the nickname of 'the Boelcke of 9b'.

In combat, Kissenberth displayed a fierce resolve, which was in full

evidence on 12 October 1916. During the famous Anglo-French raid on the Mauser factory at Oberndorf (see *Osprey Aviation Elite Units 17 - SPA124 Lafayette Escadrille* for more details), Kissenberth was one of the pilots who scrambled to intercept the bombers. Acting on his own initiative he took off in Fokker D II 540/16 and shot down two Farmans. After landing to refuel, Kissenberth again took to the air and downed an RNAS Breguet V – scoring a 'triple' for his initial victories was an incredible feat at this or any stage of the war.

KEK Ensisheim became the basis for *Jagdstaffel* 16 on 1 November 1916, and Kissenberth claimed three more victories with that unit. In August 1917 he took over *Jasta* 23b, and had brought his tally to 19 by mid May. Then on the 29th Kissenberth suffered a bad crash in a captured Sopwith Camel and was severely injured. Since his injuries prevented his return to flying, a special award of the *Pour le Mérite* was granted on 30 June 1918 (a score of 20 was generally required).

Another nascent ace who logged time in a Pfalz monoplane was Willy Rosenstein. Born of Jewish parents in Stuttgart on 28 January 1892, Rosenstein was one of the few wartime German airmen with extensive pre-war flying experience. Having gained his pilot's licence in March 1912, he was soon training German army officers to fly at the Rumpler Works at Johannisthal. Rosenstein also won several prestigious flying competitions and went on to become the Gotha firm's chief test pilot and instructor – by January 1914 he had 3000 flights under his belt.

Some months after World War 1 commenced, Rosenstein eventually wound up as a pilot with F. Fl. Abt. 19 at Porcher airfield, flying Albatros

Otto Kissenberth was a pilot with *KEK* Ensisheim when he posed with this Pfalz E I. This photograph gives a fine view of the seven-cylinder Oberursel U 0 rotary engine. Kissenberth's pince-nez and somewhat baby-faced countenance belied his fiercely determined and aggressive nature

Taken on the same occasion as the photograph above, this view of Kissenberth with his Pfalz E I at *KEK* Ensisheim reveals the circular Pfalz nameplate on the front of the cowling (an imitation of Morane-Saulnier practice). The E I was the first Pfalz product armed with a synchronised machine gun. The translucency of the bleached white fabric is evident. The multitude of national markings was perhaps deemed necessary to prevent confusion with French Morane-Saulnier machines

A relaxed Kissenberth happily poses with a perky pup in Pfalz E II 657/15 – the castor oil staining of the fuselage was very common on rotary-engined Pfalz. The E II was powered by the nine-cylinder Oberursel U I. Kissenberth did not earn any victories in Pfalz monoplanes, but he would go on to down 19 victims and command *Jasta* 23b. This indomitable airman survived the war, only to die in a climbing accident in the Bavarian Alps on 2 August 1919

two-seaters. On 22 August 1915 he collected his unit's first Fokker E I, and he flew this fighter exclusively for over two months and recorded several indecisive combats with French aircraft. Another pilot then crashed the Fokker, and in December Rosenstein began flying a brand new Pfalz E I 215/15. He flew this on five frontline flights that month, and on the 29th he attacked an aircraft and fired 20 rounds at it – he failed to bring it down, but did drive it away. This was Rosenstein's last E I flight, after which he returned to two-seaters.

He went on to fly in *Jasta* 9, then in *Jasta* 27, where he attained his first confirmed victory on 21 September 1917. Serving in *Kest* 1a, then as deputy leader of *Jasta* 40 under Carl Degelow, Rosenstein went on to raise his score to eight or nine victories by the end of the conflict.

First-hand accounts of combat flying in Pfalz E-types are scarce, but we are fortunate that Kurt Jentsch (variously credited with one to as many as seven victories) gave detailed descriptions of his experiences with the Pfalz monoplanes in his excellent book *Jagdflieger im Feuer*. Jenstch began the war as an infantryman, earning distinction on the Eastern Front until sidelined by a lung ailment from the end of January 1916 to March. He succeeded in attaining a transfer to aviation, making his first training flights at the *Fliegerschule* at Niederneuendorf. Jentsch went on to the flying school at FEA I in September, and reported to the Fokker *Militärflugschule* at the end of October 1916. There, he gained an intimate knowledge of the idiosyncrasies of the rotary-engined Fokkers.

Ordered to report to AFP 13 as a single-seat fighter pilot, Jentsch was attached to the *Kampfstaffel des Armee Flugpark* 13, which was sent to Hudova, on the Balkan front, to provide support for the Bulgarian Army. After a long and tortuous journey he arrived and made his first acquaintance with Pfalz E I 445/15 – one of three which equipped the unit. On 5 February 1916 Jenstch and his comrade Hans Schiebel made preparations to fly from the short 'air strip' beside the railway line to their new airfield at Mirovice, watched intently by a troop of curious Bulgarian soldiers. Jentsch wrote (as translated by O'Brien Browne);

Willy Rosenstein of F. Fl. Abt. 19 poses with his Pfalz E I 215/15 on *Flugplatz* Porcher in December 1915. The large display of the serial number on the aft fuselage was unusual, and must have been applied at unit level. The serial number is also painted in white on the black wheel cover. A distinguished pre-war aviator, Rosenstein had already made 3000 flights by January 1914. From F. Fl. Abt. 19 he went on to fly under Hermann Göring in *Jasta* 27, then with *Kest* 1a and finally under Carl Degelow in *Jasta* 40s. Rosenstein had claimed a total of 8/9 confirmed victories by November 1918. After the war he became an amateur racing car driver and continued to fly, but emigrated to South Africa in 1936 to escape the anti-Semitism of the Nazi regime. Rosenstein's son Ernest died whilst flying a Spitfire with the South African Air Force in 1945 (*R G Gill*)

Rosenstein's groundcrew from F. Fl. Abt. 19 pose with E I 215/15 on Porcher airfield in December 1915. The bleached fabric covering is evident – German pilot Kurt Weil recalled many years later that 'The old Aviatiks were snow white, and so, as I remember, were the first Pfalz monoplanes. These aircraft were brilliant white – so white that if you flew in sunlight, they looked transparent from the ground' (*R G Gill*)

Otto Parschau (in flying gear) was a pre-war military pilot who was a great champion of the Fokker monoplanes, and in fact helped Anthony Fokker introduce his armed Eindecker to combat units in 1915. Parschau served as a Fokker pilot in *Kampfgeschwader* 1 and then *Abwehr Kommando Nord,* and the *Pour le Mérite* was awarded to him following his eighth victory on 10 July 1916. Parschau was probably trying out the Pfalz E I seen here. Note the signal flare pistol attached to the cockpit side

Kurt Jentsch had a long and extremely varied flying career during the war, and gained his first experience in fighters flying the Pfalz E I on the Balkan/Macedonian Front. After his service there, he would go on to fly in *Jasta* 1, Fl. Abt. (A). 234 and then *Jasta* 61, where he used the Pfalz D IIIa. This view was taken close to war's end when he was a pilot in the prestigious *Jasta* 'Boelcke' of JG III

'The mechanics have been working on the assembly of the three monoplanes since the break of the new day. We are there throughout all of the work, and watch everything like hawks so that they don't make a mess of things. The Pfalz Eindecker is a copy of the French Morane monoplane. The fuselage is shorter than that of the Fokker Eindecker. Its weight is quite heavy. Two men have to expend a lot of energy to lift it. The fuselage of the Fokker Eindecker can almost be raised by one hand, that is how light (balanced) it is.

'The wings' angle of incidence is uncommonly high; in normal situations this amounts to 13 degrees. When rigging the wings (which is carried out with the aircraft in normal flight attitude), the angle of incidence of both wings must coincide, otherwise the aircraft "hangs" to one side in the air.

'Pfalz Eindecker E 445/15 is finally ready for take-off. I put on my crash helmet, pull on my furs and wedge myself into the cockpit. The chocks are in place. The first mechanic switches on the engine. It ignites with the very first swing. I hold it back – it's putting out 1180 revs. I raise my hand to show I'm ready for take-off. The chocks are removed.

'It is now 1410 hrs. I let the "blip" switch (*Schnurpsknopf*) go and give full rudder. The engine drones, and after a 15-metre taxi, the machine lifts into the air. In a flash the crate rises above the ground. Although my attention was on making a successful take-off, I also see the Bulgarian soldiers enthusiastically tossing their caps into the air.

'The Pfalz Eindecker climbs well. I have reached 1000 metres in three minutes. I see many tents standing on the left bank of the Vardar River. These must be *Feldflieger Abteilungen* 30 and 66, to whom we were attached at the depot.

'Having reached the new airfield, I switch off the engine and spiral down. I know well the responsibility that rests on my shoulders – estimate the height exactly and land smoothly. Rolling to a stop, the crate sits almost exactly in the middle of the airfield. A load has suddenly fallen from my shoulders.

'Attentively, I watch the Hudova basin. After half an hour, I see a Pfalz monoplane taking off, which soon rapidly approaches. Unfortunately, the landing goes badly. The propeller and axle are shot to Hell. Angrily, Hans Schiebel climbs out of the cockpit. I console him because I know that it is very difficult to land here.'

Several days later, Vfw Jentsch had his first encounter with the enemy;

'Evening is falling. We are sitting in front of the tents, observing the frontlines with telescopes. Suddenly, white shrapnel clouds appear. An aircraft has flown over the frontlines and is approaching the Vardar Valley. In a few minutes I am sitting in my craft and fly off. I fly southwards in order to cut off the opponent's route.

'In spite of the flak, the enemy crate continues on its way. You can follow it by the chain of shrapnel clouds that stretch out along the entire valley. I am considering taking my craft up to a great height.

'Regardless, I do not let the enemy out of sight. The enemy *aviateur* (as we in our "fliers' language" like to describe ourselves) has started to return and is flying back through the Vardar Valley. If I want to get a shot in, I'll have to get down to business. The flak in the area shows no consideration for me, but instead bangs away as lively as before. Their fire endangers me much more than the Frenchman does.

'Above Gevegeli, I reach nearly the same height as the enemy monoplane. Unfortunately, I am still 100 metres lower. In the air you can miscalculate all too easily. Apparently, it is a French Nieuport monoplane. I can clearly recognise the national markings under the wings. The colours of both cocardes flash like ox eyes. The outer ring is red, the second one white and the dot in the middle shines bright blue.

'But my craft is too slow. In an instant, the Nieuport is 100 metres ahead and pushing on toward his frontlines. Carefully, I steer my Pfalz and draw a bead on him and commence firing. I have him right in my sights. My machine gun finally fires without jamming for once. The Nieuport doesn't want to get mixed up in anything at all. The pilot puts his crate on its nose and roars downward in a dive. I dive after him, always firing. The distance he has gained on me by diving is, however, too great, so I break off the fight because I am already far over the other side of the lines. Even though I could not manoeuvre him over our sector, I am at least richer for the experience.

'Dusk's shadows rise up. It is high time I fly back. Above Gevegeli, my engine starts to puke (pilot's slang for "sputter"). I go into a glide so that I will not make a shambles of things. There is only a bit of pressure left in the fuel tank. Although I pump hard, I pull nothing out of it. Something is not right with the tank. After a few more turns, the engine comes to a standstill. No way will I make it to the Mirovice airfield. Thus, I have to make an emergency landing. Not a breeze stirs the air. My aircraft glides perfectly with a dead engine and sits like a feather in the air.

'It is rapidly turning dark. Despite this, I keep the road from Valandovo to Hudova in view. The hangars of F. Fl. Abt. 66 appear. Sadly, I won't make it to the unit's airfield. At around 400 metres away, I land smoothly right near the road.'

On 7 April Schiebel crashed another of the unit's monoplanes when his engine failed. Left on his own with the only single-seater still intact, Jentsch wrote;

The decorated wheel covers and the large '5' painted in black on the rear fuselage make this one of the few individually decorated Pfalz Eindeckers known. The proud, but unidentified, pilot and mechanic pose with their machine. The machine gun seems to have a cloth cover in place

'One day later, on 8 April, I must fly twice. At about seven o'clock in the morning I have no success. In the evening, however, I take a shot.

'Four Frenchmen are roaming about in the area of Kalinowa. Already, when I am still far off over the Doiran Lake, the flak fire is noticeable. Here and there the sky is discoloured by shrapnel clouds.

'Clouds hang over the front at a height of 2000 metres. It is not an unbroken cloud layer, for from time to time the earth can be seen. I cannot afford to lose my way, since I do not know the area too well.

'The four *Gitterschwänze* (lattice-tails, or pusher aircraft) come evenly out of the cloud bank where they have been playing hide-and-seek. I recognise the cocardes of the Frenchmen clearly. Because I am higher, I put my Pfalz on its nose and fasten on to the one in the lead over our lines. The observer shoots with his machine gun. I can clearly see him in the front of the nacelle. He accomplishes nothing because soon I am behind him. Under my machine gun fire he goes over on one wing and continually spins. Shot down!'

This Farman *may* have been confirmed as Jentsch's first victory. Eight days later he tackled a flock of six Farmans over Perdici, claiming to have sent at least two of them down, but these claims were disallowed.

A few days later, as gale force winds whipped the tent hangars and low storms clouds blackened the sky, Jentsch was ordered to take off and intercept three enemy aeroplanes over the Doiran sector. Despite his strong protests that 'I could not take any responsibility for the aircraft in such a storm', the orders stood and he managed to get under way, with predictable results. From a height of 50 metres, the Pfalz 'hit a gust of wind under the left wing which is so strong that my aeroplane somersaults' and Jentsch hit the ground in a shattering crash. Jentsch escaped with scrapes, bruises and an 'incredible headache', but E I 445/15 was a total loss.

At the end of April Jentsch received a brand new Fokker E II;

'I am boisterously happy that I finally have a Fokker! At 1030 hrs I take off on a test flight. Already the take-off was a different thing from the ponderous Pfalz. The Pfalz monoplane is about as well-suited for air combat as a cow is for playing the lute. Only heaven knows who hung these crates around the neck of the army office.'

In fact, by 17 August 1916 all Pfalz aircraft had been withdrawn from all fronts by order of the chief of field aviation due to 'the numerous fatal crashes

Ltn Walter von Bülow-Bothkamp was another eventual 'Blue Max' recipient who flew a Pfalz E II. He is seen with E II 278/15 during his early service in *Feld Flieger Abteilung* 22. Von Bülow scored his first two victories with the unit in October 1915, but they were likely obtained in a Fokker Eindecker or even an AEG G II. He went on to fly with Fl. Abt. 300 in Palestine, then as a successful *Jagdflieger* in *Jasta* 18. One of three famous flying brothers, von Bülow eventually commanded *Jasta* 36 and then the elite *Jasta* 'Boelcke' before his death in combat on 6 January 1918

in recent times'. Historian Peter M Grosz calculates that approximately 110 Pfalz E-types were destroyed and cannibalised for spares at a cost of 1.5 million marks. Production of the monoplanes stopped at the Pfalz firm, and it was proposed that the company undertake licence production of the Roland D II. The company's experience in building these streamlined biplanes would eventually help lead to the design and production of the first totally indigenous Pfalz fighter.

PFALZ D III INTO SERVICE

In September 1916 Pfalz received a contract to produce 20 Roland D I fighters under licence, and it later built 100 Roland D IIs and an identical number of D IIas. These designs utilised a complex *Wickelrumpf* or wrapped-fuselage construction, and Pfalz factory workers and engineers would also become skilled at this technique. Such a fuselage was comprised of a spare framework with a nominal number of frames and stringers. Two sturdy half-fuselage shells comprised of two layers of three-ply veneer strips were joined to the frame. After being nailed to the sub-frame, the two fuselage halves were covered in fabric and doped, producing a semi-monocoque fuselage with smooth contours.

In November 1916 the Pfalz firm hired aeronautical engineer Rudolf Geringer. Proceeding to work immediately, Geringer and his team revealed their first design in April 1917 – the sleek and elegant Pfalz D III, powered by the 160 hp Mercedes D IIIa.

Like the Albatros designers, Geringer had studied the French Nieuport sesquiplane ('one and one-half wings', with interplane 'V' struts) layout. However, instead of a single-spar lower wing, the Pfalz D III included a two-spar bottom wing with improved aeroelastic qualities. This design thus generally avoided the structural faults that plagued the Albatros sesquiplanes. Factory performance tests were announced in April. Duly impressed, *Idflieg* cancelled the current production run of licence-built Roland D IIIs and indicated that the remaining 70 aircraft to be produced should be Pfalz D III machines.

A new aircraft was always an object of intense interest. Here is Pfalz D III 1370/17, looking pristine and freshly delivered, at *Jasta* 10's airfield at Marcke. It is coming under inspection by the *Jasta* technical officer and his mechanics. The immaculate machine displays none but the factory markings at this stage, and the propeller spinner and its cap have been removed (or were not yet installed), as this D III is possibly prepared for a familiarisation flight. 1370/17 was eventually flown by Vzfw Hecht and marked with the usual chrome yellow struts, nose and wheel discs, as well as a green tail and two vertical black stripes on the fuselage (it was also *possibly* briefly flown by Werner Voss). On 27 December 1918 Hecht was brought down behind British lines by No 35 Sqn RFC, and his intact D III given the British Number 'G110'. It became the subject of many photographs and technical scrutiny – it was powered by Mercedes engine No 33321

PFALZ D III INTO SERVICE

In May 1917 the compulsory *Typenprüfung* (type test) was performed on two D IIIs at Adlershof. The test report concluded that 'The flight performance corresponds to that of the Albatros D V. The flight characteristics on the whole are good, but must be improved by a small modification to the rudder'. After some redesign, and strengthening of the wing spars and the suggested rudder changes were complete, Pfalz was allowed to proceed with the construction of 70 new D IIIs and an additional 300 ordered in June.

Idflieg reported that the initial D IIIs would 'still reach the front this month' on 24 July – the first examples were probably provided to *Jasta* 10 of *Jagdgeschwader* I in July/August for operational evaluation. Although only three Pfalz D IIIs were reported in the frontline inventory by the end of August, historian Peter M Grosz suggests this listing may have been incomplete. Sopwith Pup pilot Gordon Taylor of No 66 Sqn recalled encountering the new aircraft on 31 August;

'I watched them grow into the full shape of aeroplanes – all silver, but not the Albatros. The tailplane was different, more rectangular than the spade shape of the Albatros. They looked lighter, even slimmer than our usual opponents. They were Pfalz Scouts. It was said that they weren't as good as the Albatros. But they were obviously still much faster than our machines.'

Deliveries increased through September and October. These sleek new fighters in their overall *silbergrau* (silver-grey) finish must have elicited intense interest upon their arrival at the *Jagdstaffeln*. The speed and climb of the new aeroplane was recorded as good and both the view from the cockpit and manoeuvrability were 'excellent', but the pilots complained about the positioning of the twin machine guns. On the D III, these were buried in the fuselage just ahead of the cockpit – a holdover from the Rolands. In response to this and other demands, Pfalz brought out the redesigned D IIIa, which incorporated raised guns, a rounded tailplane of increased area and rounded lower wingtips.

The second production batch of D III types was switched to the D IIIa with 100 aircraft still to be completed. The total number of D IIIs produced amounted to about 260, while some 750 of the D IIIa were built. The types were occasionally confused even in official *Fliegertruppe* inventories, and pilots' accounts often blur the distinction between the two. It is recorded that there were 145 D IIIs in the frontline inventory by the end of October 1917 (some were mis-reported D IIIa examples) and deliveries continued apace. The number of both types at the front reached its zenith in early 1918 with 443 being reported at the end of February and 446 (mostly D IIIa) two months later. The numbers then tapered off, but the Pfalz soldiered on well into the summer.

It would seem that relatively few *Jagdstaffeln* were equipped entirely with the D III and/or the D IIIa. It is thus often difficult to determine if a certain ace's victories were actually scored in a Pfalz. This chapter will examine some of the pre-eminent *Staffeln* that flew these machines.

Jasta 10

It is perhaps indicative of the promise of the new Pfalz D III that one of the very first units to receive it was *Jasta* 10 of the prestigious JG I, the

A stellar cluster of VIPs discuss the merits of the Pfalz D III at *Jasta* 10. The officer second from left is thought to be Hptm Curt Schwarzenberger, who was *Referent* for fighter development at *Idflieg*. Third from left is the diminutive *Staffelführer* Ltn d R Hans Klein (ironically, *Klein* translates as small or little), who would gain the last of his 22 victories in *Jasta* 10. The officer directly beneath the propeller spinner (with its cap removed) is thought to be Ltn d R Max Kühn (three victories). Fifth from left is a nattily attired Ernst Eversbusch, co-owner of the Pfalz company. Sixth from left is the *Staffel* veteran Aloys Heldmann, then an unknown airman. The D III in the background boasts the full display of the *Jasta* 10 yellow colour on its nose, wheels and struts, as usual rendered a very dark tone by the orthochromatic film in use. The two dark stripes seen on the top wing may well have been formation leader's markings. Auxiliary wire bracing was installed on the wingtips of this Pfalz - a common practice designed to prevent the bending or excessive deflection of the upper wingtips during combat, which many pilots had noticed. Taking a leaf from Anthony Fokker's handbook, Ernst Eversbusch tried to maintain close relations with frontline pilots and to promote his product at the same time. The diaries of several units record lavish presents from Pfalz – on 22 December 1917, for instance, *Jasta* 24 received a Christmas gift of 300 marks for the groundcrew and a case of wine for the officers

'Richthofen' *Geschwader*. *Jasta* 10 would become closely associated with the type, and its yellow-nosed machines are familiar to many enthusiasts. Among the four component units of JG I (*Jastas* 4,6,10 and 11), only *Staffeln* 10 and 4 would be equipped primarily with the D III and D IIIa, although *Jasta* 11 had a few. *Jasta* 10 was based at Marcke, near Courtrai, in the German 4. *Armee*, and in September 1917 was commanded by the mercurial Ltn d R Werner Voss. The unit's opposition in the Flanders skies included some of the best airmen the Royal Flying Corps (RFC) had to offer.

Voss had been hand-picked for the helm of *Jasta* 10 by von Richthofen, and he took over on 30 July. He was now in command of the lowest-scoring unit (to this date) in JG I. In his *Geschwader* history (*Jagd in Flanderns Himmel*), JG I adjutant Karl Bodenschatz described Voss as 'very young, wiry, with 34 victories behind him, and the *Orden Pour le Mérite*. This Daredevil First Class, who is sliding around on his chair like a lively schoolboy'. When interviewed by historian Alex Imrie in 1961, Voss' mechanic Karl Timm recalled that he followed the ace from *Jasta* 5 to *Jasta* 10 to 'maintain his Pfalz D III. This machine was not popular, and Voss only scored four victories with it before he received the Fokker Triplane'.

Voss certainly flew a Pfalz (along with an Albatros D V) at *Jasta* 10, but it is nearly impossible to confirm that he scored four victories on the type. From his arrival at the unit until his first victory in Fokker F I 103/17 on 3 September, Voss did indeed claim four victims, but the aircraft he flew while doing so is not recorded.

Voss was flying his Triplane on 5 September when, along with Ltn Löwenhardt, he completely out-flew a patrol of Pups from No 46 Sqn. Sopwiths were credited to both Voss (his 40th victory) and Löwenhardt (his 3rd). Löwenhardt (also spelled Loewenhardt) was apparently flying an Albatros that day, but he would likely utilise the Pfalz to attain some of his succeeding victories.

Born in Breslau on 7 April 1897, Löwenhardt went to war as an infantryman aged 17, and received honours on several fronts. After serving as a pilot in F. Fl. Abt. (A) 265, he joined *Jasta* 10 in March 1917.

His first victories came slowly, but after his third success his skills came into focus. Löwenhardt began to earn a reputation as a balloon-buster, and gasbags made up eight of his first 14 victories. In June 1918, after he had won his 'Blue Max', he chanced to meet the mother of Manfred von

Geschwader Kommandeur von Richthofen (fourth from right) pays a visit to the men of his *Jasta* 10. They are, from left to right, Paul Aue (10 victories), Julius Bender, Aloys Heldmann (15), Justus Grassmann (10), *Jasta* 10 commander Erich Löwenhardt (54 victories, with his usual close-cropped hair), *Geschwader* Adjutant Karl Bodenschatz with dachshund, Max Kühn (3), von Richthofen, *Jasta* 10 technical officer Friedrich Schäfer, 'Fritz' Friedrichs (21) and Alfons Nitsche. Richthofen's knobbed walking stick, the famous *Geschwaderstock*, is stuck into the ground just in front of Aue. The star performers Löwenhardt and Friedrichs would both meet accidental ends, undefeated by the enemy. Friedrichs died on 15 July 1918 when the unstable phosphorus ammunition in his Fokker D VII auto-ignited – he took to his parachute, but the harness and shroud lines became entangled with the Fokker's tail and the ace fell to his death. Löwenhardt was killed on 10 August when his D VII collided with that of Alfred Wentz of *Jasta* 11. Both pilots bailed out but Löwenhardt's parachute failed to open properly

Richthofen on a train as he was going to visit his widowed mother. The Baroness recorded her own view of the famed *Jagdflieger*;

'We started up a conversation, his serious well-chiseled soldier's face came alive. So many beneficial things came out of this amiable, honest man, who had already carried out so many praiseworthy deeds as a ski troop leader in the icy Carpathians, in the Dolomites, the Balkans and later as an observer and fighter pilot. Now he wanted to go home, as Manfred once did, in order to stand before his mother in the adornment of the *Pour le Mérite*.'

On 7 September 1917 a newcomer arrived at *Jasta* 10 – Jewish pilot Vfw Friedrich Rüdenberg, who had experienced air combat as a member of Fl. Abt. (A) 259. He would later recall Voss as, 'totally fearless. Militarily he had the weakness of being an absolute loner. Often, he separated from his *Staffel* over the front, and he did not train us very systematically.'

NCO pilot Paul Aue, with five victories credited, was wounded on 19 September, and his skill would be missed. He wrote 'On 19 September 1917 I was wounded in combat with 24 Britishers at 3000 metres near Roulers – three bullets, one of them explosive'. The next day, as the Battle of Menin Road Ridge erupted, Löwenhardt suffered a minor wound. He was back in action 24 hours later when he and Ltn d R Gustav Bellen flamed a balloon each – the first score for Bellen.

On the fateful evening of the 23rd, Voss took off in his Dr I, accompanied by Bellen and Rüdenberg, both apparently flying Pfalz. A second *Kette* (flight) of three aircraft took off, led by Oblt Ernst Weigand. Rüdenberg would write;

It has long been claimed that this poor quality photograph shows a *Jasta* 10 Pfalz D III that had just been landed by Werner Voss. The nose displays the early, less extensive yellow paint job seen on a few other early *Staffel* 10 Pfalz, such as in the photo of Voss and his brothers on page 22. The struts and wheel covers have not as yet been painted in the *Jasta* colour. The two vertical stripes on either side of the fuselage cross were probably black. The serial number cannot, of course, be discerned, but the similarity of the fuselage markings to those seen on the famous photographs of Hecht's 1370/17 suggest that this *may* have been that same D III prior to the application of further markings. Sadly, confirmation of the Voss identification for this D III is lacking

The *Jasta* 10 *Staffelführer* Werner Voss (at left) was visited by his brothers Otto and Max on 23 September 1917. The photographs taken on that occasion were the last ever recorded of Voss, for a few hours later he was dead. That very morning he had downed a DH 4 for his 48th, and final, victory, and it may be that this image shows him in his somewhat grimy sweater worn during that flight. According to his friend Paul Bäumer, Voss could often be found in the hangars working on his aircraft alongside the mechanics, wearing an oily drill jacket. Seen in the background is a yellow-nosed Pfalz D III of *Jasta* 10 with the spinner cap clearly in place and fabric covers over the propeller blades

Hans Klein (left) poses with a Pfalz D III which is traditionally believed to be his, marked with a lengthwise dark stripe. The cockpit occupant may be Hptm Schwarzenberger, but the officer at right with the cavalry spurs is unidentified. In Osprey *Aviation Elite Units 16 - Jagdgeschwader Nr I 'Richthofen's Circus'*, this D III was tentatively depicted with the longitudinal stripe rendered in yellow. The author now believes this marking was a different colour, probably black. A small fuselage patch may be noted extending into the stripe beneath the cockpit. Its cabane struts are certainly chrome yellow, however (*L Bronnenkant*)

'In the evening we flew again to the front with Voss. Again he left us – never to return. He flew a special machine that did not allow us to catch up with him.'

As he had done before, Voss out-distanced his wingmen in his Tri-plane. This time, however, he flew on alone to his storied and fatal clash with No 56 Sqn.

After Voss' death his former deputy Weigand became acting *Staffelführer*. Weigand was 'a very nice comrade, but with little ability to be a *Jagdstaffel* commander on the Flanders front', recalled Rüdenberg. Only two days after Voss fell Weigand led a mixed formation of Pfalz and Albatros over the Houthulst Forest, Rüdenberg among them;

'We met three English fighters about 200-300 metres above us. Their leader was an exemplary fighter pilot. He was a loner, like Voss, and attacked all by himself, his companions only had to keep his tail clean.'

The superb SE 5a pilot from No 56 Sqn was Lt Leonard Barlow, who swooped down and shot Weigand's Albatros into flaming pieces with a

head-on attack. Barlow then zoomed away to riddle the Pfalz of Uffz Werkmeister with a burst and sent the D III down with dense smoke streaming away. These were black times for the *Jasta*.

Luckily for the *Staffel* its next CO was seasoned and accomplished *Jagdflieger* Ltn d R Hans Klein. Born on 17 January 1891 in Stettin, in Pomerania, Klein left his classes at the Charlottenburg Technical College when war broke out. Serving in the infantry, he quickly gained a commission and transferred to aviation in February 1916. The aggressive courage he displayed in the single-seater detachment of F. Fl. Abt. 43 led to a posting to *Jasta* 4. There Klein downed 16 opponents in less than four months, but he had been wounded on 13 July 1917. Now the ace had returned to take over *Jasta* 10, and he would do so in exemplary fashion, as reported by von Richthofen;

'He is one of my most successful and best-qualified *Staffel* leaders. His courageous gallantry, vigorous aggressive spirit and relentless daring know no bounds. As a leader in the air, an ideal example of courage and bravery (who) requires of his subordinates the exertion of all strengths and relentless determination. He was concerned about the well-being of every one of his men.'

The thick morning fog of 2 October had cleared when Klein led a group of *Jasta* 10 Pfalz and Albatros scouts to intercept bombers of No 55 Sqn that had attacked Marcke. Klein opened his new account by knocking down DH 4 A7642 for his 17th claim. Rüdenberg was also aloft, in a substitute Pfalz since his other one had been damaged;

'My first mechanic had neglected to tell me that he had not filled the reserve fuel tank. When the English saw us, they turned north to cross Dutch territory to reach the Schelde estuary and the Channel. They also split up into several groups. The flight had been long, and my motor suddenly made the noise that meant a lack of fuel. The main tank was empty, and I switched to the reserve tank, but without success – the propeller stopped.'

Rüdenberg attempted to glide down for a landing, but crashed badly. When he regained consciousness, he found himself upside down in what remained of his Pfalz – the fuselage had broken off just aft of the cockpit and in front, but the sturdy shell around him had remained intact. He emerged with severe bruises and sprains, but he was better off than his comrade Ltn Max Römer. Rüdenberg claimed that Römer had lost contact with the others, and his Pfalz – still a relatively unfamiliar

Friedrich Rüdenberg was no ace, but his recently uncovered memoirs provide some unique glimpses of life in *Jasta* 10. His Pfalz D III (probably 1371/17) displayed a diagonal fuselage sash and chordwise stripes on the vertical and horizontal tail surfaces. A signal flare pistol was affixed to the starboard side of the cockpit. After flying the Fokker D VII in *Jasta* 75, Rüdenberg survived the war. He later emigrated to Israel

The details are unknown, but at some point the D III thought to be Klein's (seen on page 22) was damaged in this accident. This view shows that the lengthwise stripe was darker than the chrome yellow nose colour, and in fact extended onto the painted nose section. The patch underneath the cockpit can still be seen here. The struts, wheel covers and *perhaps* the tail surfaces were also yellow. Auxiliary wingtip bracing cables may be noted (*R Kastner*)

In one of a series of publicity photos taken with his Pfalz D III 1395/17, Ltn d R Heldmann strikes a relaxed pose on the wheel. A detail of this shot was used as number 664 in the well-known series of Sanke postcards of famous airmen. This D III was one of the few early production machines which was terrain camouflaged on all uppersurfaces in two or more colours – either in lilac and green or reddish-brown and green. Note that the colours were applied to the interplane and cabane struts, and that the weights table and other factory-stencilled data was applied over the camouflage. When interviewed late in life, Heldmann recalled that the wheel covers were white, but they may have been a light blue instead – a colour Heldmann used as a personal display on the tail sections of several other aircraft. None of the unit's usual yellow markings have yet been applied

Heldmann nonchalantly puffs on a cigarette as he prepares for a sortie in D III 1395/17. Waiting obediently behind him with a flying coat is Heldmann's *Bursche* (orderly), while an oil-stained mechanic gives the pilot his goggles. The underside of the Pfalz's fuselage was not camouflaged, but was either typical silver-grey or possibly light blue. Note the serial number stencilling aft of the fuselage cross. Heldmann made it through the war with 15 victories, and lived to become one of the last survivors of the Richthofen *Geschwader*

aeroplane on the front – had been shot down by a pilot from another *Jasta* who failed to recognise the type.

The proficient duo of Klein and Löwenhardt continued to rack up claims through October, the CO getting two Sopwiths to take his total to 19 and the latter torching yet another balloon on the 14th. On the morning of the 18th, the weather cleared to permit a four-machine *Kette* from the *Staffel*, along with aircraft from *Jastas* 3 and 7, to tackle two large groups of RFC bombers and escorts heading to Ingelmunster. Klein and Löwenhardt each brought down a Bristol from No 22 Sqn, the crew of Löwenhardt's (2Lt B B Perry and CH Bartlett) being taken PoW and given a friendly tour of Marcke airfield by the *Jasta* 10 pilots.

The British tank assault at Cambrai broke through the German lines on 20 November, and JG I was hastily transferred north to the imperiled front. The four *Staffeln* were soon in place at airfields around Avesnes-le-Sec, with *Jasta* 10 located at Iwuy. On the 29th the clearing weather brought fighters of both sides out, and Klein and his wingman, Ltn d R Aloys (also spelled Alois) Heldmann, both claimed Sopwiths shot down near Crevecoeur. The reliable Heldmann, a *Jasta* veteran, was flying his yellow-nosed Pfalz D III 4117/17 marked with a blue tail.

In preparation for a German counter-attack, *Jasta* 10 moved to Avesnes-le-Sec on 29 November. The last day of the month ushered in a furious and successful assault on the ground and chaotic combat in the air – JG I flew 103 sorties and claimed six RFC aircraft. The first of these was a balloon west of Ribécourt, incinerated by Klein at 1230 hrs. Just over three hours later, a patrol from *Jasta* 10 clashed with Camels near Bourlon Wood. Löwenhardt sent one of these down to crash, but this was balanced by the death of 25-year-old Ltn d R Friedrich Demandt. His

Pfalz D III 4116/17 was shot down by Lt G E Thomson of No 46 Sqn for the third of his eventual 21 victories. The wreckage of Demandt's machine was one of the first Pfalz to fall into British hands, and the reports of this silver D III indicate that it had a yellow tail as a personal insignia, as well as the standard yellow nose, wheel covers and struts.

The 7 December saw the British withdraw from Bourlon, ending the Battle of Cambrai. The pace of aerial conflict slackened off in the worsening winter weather, but on the 27th Vfw Hecht flew into the overcast skies in his green-tailed Pfalz D III 1370/17. The inexperienced airman was shot down by the crew of an Armstrong Whitworth FK 8 of No 35 Sqn, but the German pilot brought his D III down to a smooth landing at Vermand. The first Pfalz to fall into British hands totally intact was numbered 'G 110', and it came under intense scrutiny.

The *Jasta* 10 pilots continued to fly their Pfalz and Albatros into January's grey skies, no doubt regarding the nimble Fokker Dr I triplanes of *Jasta* 6 and 11 with envy. On the morning of the 18th a patrol of *Jastas* 6 and 10 pilots braved the mist and storms to attack a formation of British two-seaters and scouts. Löwenhardt was credited with a Bristol to bring his score to 10, making him a *Kanone* ('cannon', or ace) by German standards. Once again, however, the victory triumph was marred by loss. No 54 Sqn's Maj R S Maxwell was attacked by Flg Helmuth Riensberg in his Pfalz D III 4059/17. Maxwell turned beneath the path of the enemy's dive, and later reported;

'EA (enemy aircraft) continued diving followed by (my) Camel. After a burst at about 70 yards, EA turned over and right bottom wing came partly away and folded back. EA went down in spiral.'

Jasta 10 suffered a critical loss on 19 February. Hans Klein had received the highly anticipated telegram announcing his *Pour le Mérite* on 5 December and had continued to lead his *Staffel* through the winter skies in his Pfalz, bringing his score to 22. Bodenschatz wrote that on the 19th, Klein landed his D IIIa 4283/17 on the *Jasta* airfield and 'clambers out of his machine, badly upset – the index finger of his right hand had been shot off during air combat, and he has to go to Field Hospital No 23'. He had taken a flesh wound to the right arm as well, and his combat flying days were over. Klein would return to JG I as a staff officer later in 1918.

On 8 March, Ltn d R Heldmann – this time in an Albatros D V – made his fourth claim in the *Staffel* record. *Jasta* 10 had joined *Staffeln* 8 and 17 in intercepting a flight of French Breguet bombers over Fresnoy le Grand. Heldmann claimed two from *Escadrille* BR 107, but had only one confirmed.

The 22-year-old Heldmann came from Grevenbroich, near Köln, and was a pilot of varied experience. After serving as an infantryman in Russia, he switched to aviation and flew two-seaters in F. Fl. Abt. 59 and 57 on the Serbian, Bulgarian and Western fronts. He came to *Jasta* 10 from Fl. Abt. (A) 256 and chalked

Ltn d R Hans Klein is seen (third from left) some time during his recovery from the wounds he sustained on 19 February 1918. Klein's Pfalz D IIIa was hit by a burst that took off his right index finger, and he suffered a flesh wound in the arm as well. The location and date of this photograph is not recorded, but it may well have been taken at FEA (*Flieger Ersatz Abteilung*) 9, where Klein went after his hospital stay ended on 17 March 1918. The other personnel are unidentified, as is the Halberstadt CL II two-seater in the background. In late April Klein was posted to the *Jasta* 10 *Stab* (staff), and finished the war in that capacity. Along with Ernst Udet, he made at least one trip to the Pfalz Works at Speyer to inspect the new Pfalz D XII and D VIII. Klein gained an engineering degree after the war and joined the Luftwaffe in 1935 as a major. Eventually he attained the rank of major-general, and was Deputy Commander of all Luftwaffe fighters before he died on 18 November 1944 (*L Bronnenkant*)

Ltn d R Justus Grassmann is seen in the cockpit of his *Jasta* 10 D IIIa. Grassmann achieved all ten of his victories in a D VII, but he certainly flew the Pfalz in combat. He had entered the war in a field artillery regiment, and saw action in Poland and Kurland. Following transfer to the *Fliegertruppe,* Grassmann flew long-distance observation missions in DFW and Rumpler two-seaters in Fl. Abt. 32. Late in his life he wrote to historian A E Ferko;

'I arrived, via the Valenciennes *Jagdfliegerschule,* at *Jasta* 10 of the Richthofen *Jagdgeschwader* in October 1917 and remained there until the end of the war. I flew Fokker D VIIs, while we still had Pfalz D III in the winter of 1917-18. The aircraft (D VII) of Löwenhardt, the *Staffelführer,* was painted completely yellow. The markings on my own aircraft were brown and white striped elevators, including the surfaces of the stabilisers'

up his first confirmed victory on 22 July when he downed an RE 8, followed by a SPAD a week later.

Heldmann would finish the war as a 15-victory ace, receive the Knight's Cross with Swords of the Royal Hohenzollern House Order (generally known as 'the Hohenzollern'), and twice serve as acting commander of the *Staffel.*

By early March massive preparations were underway for Germany's upcoming great offensive in the west, code-named Operation *Michael,* and later generally referred to as the *Kaiserschlacht.* On the evening of 12 March, Löwenhardt demonstrated the balloon-busting skills *Jasta* 10 was becoming famous for. Clearly emerging as the *Staffel* leader in the air, he and his comrade Ltn d R Bohlein each 'fried sausages' west of La Bassée.

On the 18th, *Jasta* 10 cooperated with *Staffeln* 6 and 11 in the famous 'air battle of Le Cateau', as large numbers of aircraft tangled in a sprawling dogfight in which JG I felled nine opponents – Löwenhardt successfully claimed a two-seater for his 13th. Two days later, on the eve of the great offensive, the Pfalz and Albatros pilots of *Staffel* 10 flew to the advance landing field at Awoingt in utter secrecy and quickly pushed their machines into tent hangars.

On 21 March the massive German assault erupted at 0945 hrs. The JG I pilots, dressed and ready for take-off, stood angrily staring into a dense grey wall of fog. *Jasta* 'Löwenhardt', as *Staffel* 10 was now informally known, had been ordered to perform its specialty by attacking the British balloon line at 1000 hrs. Thick mists prevented this, but less than three hours later Löwenhardt and his *Staffel* mate Ltn d R Friedrichs flew their Pfalz off into the murk to attack two balloons reported up at Ruyalcourt and Fins. By 1300 hrs they were both confirmed as destroyed, one of them being the first score for the soon-to-be renowned 'balloon killer' Friedrichs (although there was only a single balloon lost, probably Löwenhardt's).

Born on 21 February 1895, Friedrich 'Fritz' Friedrichs had been headed for a medical career when the war broke out. Commissioned in the 2. *Thüringisches Infanterie-Regt* Nr 32, he had served on the Western and Serbian fronts. His left leg was wounded so badly that he was judged unfit for further infantry service. However, still eager to serve, Friedrichs attended both observer and pilot schools in early 1917 and joined F. Fl. Abt. (A) 264 in June of that year.

He arrived at *Jasta* 10 on 11 January 1918 and had unsuccessfully claimed a Camel in the titanic brawl of 18 March. On the 27th Friedrichs was part of a large JG I formation that headed off a group of DH 4 bombers and their Bristol F 2B escorts. His mentor Löwenhardt spattered a de Havilland from No 25 Sqn with bursts, sending it down in flames for his 15th *Luftsieg.* About an hour later Friedrichs achieved his second confirmed 'kill' when he brought an SE 5a of No 40 Sqn down behind the German lines – part of JG I's impressive total of 13 for the day.

The airmen of *Jasta* 10 struggled on through the waning offensive in their inferior machines. Löwenhardt was now the commander of the *Staffel*, and its only scorer in April, accounting for two RAF fighters to take his unit's total past 60. On 2 May he dealt a blow to the morale of No 56 Sqn when that celebrated unit's commander, Maj R Balcombe-Brown, fell to his guns. The next day Paul Aue (back in action after his September wounds) showed he had not lost his touch when he brought a 'Brisfit' of No 48 Sqn down in German territory, and Friedrichs added a DH 9 for his third victory. The succeeding day the dependable Heldmann achieved 'acedom' by destroying an SE5a of No 24 Sqn.

The first examples of the much-anticipated Fokker D VIIs began to arrive at *Jasta* 10 in early May. In the coming weeks the old Pfalz were phased out and *Jasta* 10 entered a new era.

Jasta 4

As the other *Staffel* in JG I primarily equipped with the Pfalz, the experiences of *Jasta* 4 parallel those of *Jasta* 10 somewhat. However, *Staffel* 4 had a far more distinguished record of 80 victories by early September 1917, when the first D IIIs arrived to augment the unit's Albatros equipment. Its CO was Oblt Kurt-Bertram von Döring, a 28-year-old former dragoon officer who had transferred to aviation in June 1913 and completed his pilot's training a year later. He became *Jasta* 4's leader in 'Bloody April' 1917 and had downed his sixth opponent on 3 September.

That same month the unit's groundcrew began preparing the D IIIs for combat operations, but not without setbacks. On 20 September the *Staffel* airfield at Marcke was bombed by Martinsydes of No 27 Sqn, the *Jasta* losing four mechanics killed and another wounded, three aircraft destroyed and five more badly damaged. It is not recorded how many of these were Albatros or Pfalz, but the losses put pressure on the harried groundcrew to ready newly-arrived D IIIs for action. Tragedy struck again two days later when a groundcrewman of *Jasta* 4 was accidentally wounded during the test firing of the machine guns on a new Pfalz.

On 23 September – the day Voss fell – Döring received credit for a 'Sopwith' shot down north of Ypres. The following day a Camel flown by Flt Sub-Lt Foster of No 10 Sqn, RNAS, was forced down behind German lines, apparently the victim of *Jasta* 4's 'hottest property' in this period – 19-year-old Kurt Wüsthoff. The ambitious teenager went on a veritable rampage in September, accounting for 14 RFC aircraft to bring his score to 21. He may have flown a Pfalz occasionally, but photos and other evidence indicates that he generally favoured the Albatros.

One *Jasta* 4 ace that flew a Pfalz D III was Oblt Oskar Freiherr von Boenigk, a Silesian nobleman born

Oblt Oskar Freiherr von Boenigk first flew the Pfalz D III with *Jasta* 4 in the autumn of 1917, and may well have operated the D IIIa after he took over *Jasta* 21s. His D III 1396/17 seen here displays the black ribbon marking of *Jasta* 4 wrapped around the silver grey fuselage. The lower wings of many silver Pfalz aircraft seem to appear darker than the fuselages in most photographs, which is likely an optical effect. However, the lower port wing of 1396/17 certainly *seems* to have been painted a dark glossy colour in this shot. Note that both left and right lower corners of this print have been 'cropped' by the diagonal tape fasteners that secured the photograph in its album. Thus, that is *not* a silver section of the lower wing seen in the lower left corner. This lower port wing may have been painted in a personal colour, or perhaps it is a replacement from a terrain-camouflaged D III. Photographs of other *Jasta* 4 Pfalz show the tail and sometimes the spinner painted in the pilot's personal colour – if von Boenigk did this, he may have used the yellow of his former *Grenadier Regt Nr 11 König Friedrich III*

on 25 August 1893. An army cadet at the age of 11, von Boenigk was commissioned in a grenadier regiment in 1912. Twice wounded on the Western Front, he switched to the air service and first flew as an observer in *Kasta* S.II and *Schutzstaffel* 19, then learned to fly in April 1917. Posted to *Jasta* 4 on 15 June, he wasted little time and opened his score sheet with a Sopwith downed on 20 July. On 3 September von Boenigk had claimed two more of the ubiquitous 'Sopwiths', receiving credit for one of them to bring his total to four. He 'made ace' on the 9th when he added one of the vaunted Sopwith Triplanes to his tally. His star on the rise, von Boenigk was given command of *Jasta* 21 on the last day of October.

November saw few successes gained by *Jasta* 4, with merely three victories claimed – all by the aggressive young Wüsthoff. During the German counter-attack at Cambrai on the 30th, the crowded aerial activity resulted in tragedy. In his *Jasta* 4 Pfalz, 21-year-old Ltn Wilhelm Schultze collided with the Albatros D V of 14-victory ace Ltn d R Rudolf Wendelmuth of *Jasta* 20 and both men died. Schultze was a veteran pilot of *Jasta* 4 who had claimed his first victory in August.

Little was accomplished during the winter lull of 1917/18. On 10 February 1918 (two weeks past his 20th birthday) Kurt Wüsthoff wrote to his mother, 'Since yesterday, Rittmeister von Döring has gone on leave and I am leading the *Staffel*. I am very well. A bit of a headache!' The 'headache' may refer to the responsibilities of command, for which he was ill suited – he had already spent time in a sanatorium for stomach disorders and frayed nerves. *Jasta* 11 ace Hans Georg von der Osten later recalled that the youngster alienated his *Jasta* 4 comrades because of his 'cheeky' way and unsympathetic manner;

'So von Richthofen relieved him as *Staffel* commander. I became his successor on 16 March 1918, and I had to get used to the Pfalz D III again after the grand Triplane. Von Richthofen himself gave me the order to take over the command of *Staffel* 4. I enjoyed this very much, as there were grand chaps in that *Staffel* – Ltns Rouselle, Koepsch, Maushake, Drekmann and my good pal Ltn ("Carlos") Meyer, who had been transferred in the meantime from *Jasta* 11 to *Jasta* 4, and most of all my regimental comrades Ltn Graf von Gluszewski and Ltn Graf Rautter. Both had come into the *Staffel* as their first assignments. Gluszewski had gained some two or three victories and flew till the end of the war. Rautter, in his first four weeks, could not score any victories, but then within a short time he shot down ten Englishmen. Very soon afterwards he was killed himself.'

This was Viktor von Pressentin *genannt* von Rautter, a 21-year-old former member of the prestigious 3. *Garde-Ulanen-Regt.* On 28 March he started off his victory skein by downing the Camel of seven-victory ace Lt R J Owen of

Ltn d R Karl 'Carlos' Meyer of Jasta *4 is seen posing with the tail of a Pfalz D IIIa in February 1918 at Lieu St Amand airfield. The D IIIa may or may not have been his own personal aircraft, but it displays a tail section painted in an unknown dark colour as an individual insignia. What appears to be a chordwise stripe in an even darker colour is painted on the horizontal surfaces, and the beginning of the* Jasta *marking of a black ribbon is visible. 'Carlos' Meyer was born in Caracas, of a German father and Venezuelan mother. He was a popular and reliable pilot in both* Jagdstaffeln *11 and 4, surviving the war with four victories (*HAC/UTD*)*

This unidentified Pfalz D III boasted the black spiral ribbon marking of *Jagdstaffel* 4. The spinner may have been painted white as a personal embellishment. The sharply angular tips of the lower wing and tailplane, as well as the machine gun seen buried underneath the fuselage deck just above the Axial propeller, all serve to differentiate this D III from its successor the D IIIa

The camera captures another unidentified Pfalz D IIIa of Jasta 4. This aircraft boasted both *Staffel* and individual markings. The *Jasta* marking of the black ribbon is in full display, and the black stripes on the fin and tailplane/elevators served as a personal emblem. According to a study of another photograph of this same machine, the serial number may have been 8131/17

No 43 Sqn, the British pilot becoming a PoW. Von Rautter would quickly add 14 more claims before he fell on 31 May.

In the same earlier combat that gave von Rautter his first victory, von der Osten's career came to an end, as he later recounted;

'In a scrap on 28 March I was shot down in a dogfight with a Britisher and my aeroplane was battered to pieces on the ground. We never found out why. I was flying a Pfalz D III, not an Albatros as is stated by Bodenschatz. Alas, it was a Pfalz, and these Pfalz had a nasty habit of slipping in a turn, so it can be assumed that I crashed while slipping in a turn. The aeroplane was smashed, so I don't know whether the Britisher shot it to pieces or whether I just slipped and crashed. I had a fracture of the base of the skull and a splinter fracture of the right shin, so I don't remember anything about my last air battle.'

Another young nobleman who honed his skills as a Pfalz pilot in *Jasta* 4 at this time was Raven Freiherr von Barnekow, born on 10 March 1897. He had joined the elite 2. *Garde-Ulanen-Regiment* in 1914 and learned to fly in 1917. After serving in Fl. Abt. 20, he arrived at *Jasta* 4 on 17 November and became a protégé of von Döring, as well as a good friend of Ernst Udet. The fair-haired, blue-eyed von Barnekow no doubt cut a dashing figure with the ladies in his elegant Guards uniform. Von der Osten recalled;

'Then there was Ltn Raven von Barnekow. He obtained many victories, He came from a very well-to-do family, and was an unbelievably spoiled young man.'

Although he did not score in *Jasta* 4, von Barnekow would go on to fly the Pfalz D IIIa in *Jasta* 20 and rack up five of an eventual 11 victories there.

After von der Osten's injury, command of *Jasta* 4 went to Ltn d R Johann Janzen, a former hussar from *Jasta* 6 who had thus far attained four of his eventual 13 victories. Later, he recalled;

'I was given the leadership of *Jasta* 4, whose *Staffelführer* had been badly injured. The change that I made was not a good one, since *Jasta* 4 still used the old Pfalz D III(a), while in *Jasta* 6 we had been flying the Fokker Triplane for some time. As a result of flying the Pfalz D III, which in their aged state

Although he attained no victories in *Jasta* 4, Raven Erik Henning Angus Freiherr von Barnekow would score 11 times in *Jagdstaffeln* 20 and 1. Von Barnekow had joined the prestigious 2. *Garde-Ulanen Regiment* and was commissioned on 3 March 1915. Around May 1915 he switched to the 4. *Garde-Regiment zu Fuss*. Having transferred to aviation, von Barnekow then arrived at *Jasta* 4 on 17 November 1917. He is seen here being assisted with his heavy flying boots while he dismounts from his D IIIa 42XX/17. The black ribbon emblem of the *Staffel* is clearly evident on both Pfalz in view

A lone *Jasta* 4 Pfalz D IIIa is pictured outside a tent hangar on the advance landing ground at Awoingt. *Jagdgeschwader* I had moved its entire complement of aircraft to this site on 20 March, just before the great offensive code-named Operation *Michael*. This Pfalz seems to have had its tail and possibly its nose painted a light colour to identify the pilot (*HAC/UTD*)

Pfalz D III 4059/17 was flown by Ltn d R Heinrich Arntzen of *Jasta* 15, and it is seen here having its engine run up in late 1917. Arntzen had previously served as a photographer and observer with distinction, thus he chose to use the Prussian observer's badge as a personal marking. This insignia also appeared on an Albatros D V he flew in *Jasta* 15, and later on his *Jasta* 50 OAW-built Albatros D III. On 23 December Arntzen was transferred to the command of the newly forming *Jasta* 50, where he would score the last five of his eleven victories. He received the Knight's Hohenzollern with Swords on 29 March 1918. Arntzen's career as a fighter pilot ended when he received a grievous head wound during a balloon attack on 27 May 1918, but he made it back to German lines. The ace would lose an eye, and according to one source, a piece of shrapnel was removed from his skull – which he kept as a souvenir! (*HAC/UTD*)

could reach an altitude of about 3000 metres only, where they were invariably pounced upon by a bunch of cheeky SE5s, the *Staffel* scored only three victories in April. I myself was unable to score any, despite intensive patrol work, but at the same time we were lucky not to lose any pilots.'

In fact the *Jasta* was able to account for five enemy aircraft in April. Two of these went to von Rautter, who became acting CO on 4 May. By that time his pilots had bid good riddance to their Pfalz as they re-equipped with the Dr I on 20 April. The tale of the Pfalz in JG I had come to an end.

Jasta 15/18

The history of the Pfalz in *Jagdgeschwader* Nr II (*Staffeln* 12, 13, 15 and 19) centres on the famous *Jasta* 15. However, the history of *Staffel* 15 is

This splendid view provides a close look at Ltn d R Hans Müller with his Pfalz D III 1416/17 of *Jasta* 15. Müller's usual personal emblem was the black/white diagonally striped fuselage band, here picked out by narrow black(?) borders. As with Arntzen's D III 4059/17, the pilot's individual insignia was painted over the cross on the fuselage, and there was apparently no unit marking for *Jasta* 15 in force at this time. Müller's personal black and white stripes were also applied chevron-style to the tailplane and elevators, just as they were on his later Fokker Dr I. An anemometer type ASI is affixed to the port interplane strut. This pristine D III clearly displays all the usual factory stencilling and Pfalz company logos (*courtesy M Thiemeyer*)

schizophrenically joined with that of another proficient unit, *Jasta* 18, and their stories cannot easily be told separately.

Jasta 15 received its first examples of the Pfalz D III as early as October 1917, when it was based at Le Clos Ferme in the 7. *Armee* front. Commanded by Ltn Hans von Budde, the *Staffel* never had a full complement of Pfalz but flew a typical mixed bag. One budding ace who saw action in the D III with the unit was 23-year-old Ltn d R Heinrich Arntzen, who gained his first four victories as an observer in 1916.

After learning to fly, he was posted to *Jasta* 15 in July 1917, and would also serve as the *Staffel* technical officer. A French Caudron destroyed on 13 August brought his score to five. Arntzen *may* have been flying his D III when he flamed a French balloon at Cerny-les-Bucy on 15 October for his sixth victim, but he would not score again before 23 December when he took over *Jasta* 50 – there, he would bring his total to 11.

Another Pfalz flier in *Jasta* 15 was Ltn d R Hans Müller. After flying with Fl. Abt. (A) 208, he arrived at *Jasta* 15 on 4 July 1917 – a day after his 21st birthday. He did not achieve his first successes until January 1918, when he despatched two French Paul Schmitt two-seaters.

On 2 February, JG II was formed under the leadership of Hauptmann Adolf Ritter von Tutschek, and Müller was able to switch to Fokker Dr Is now that *Jasta* 15 was part of an elite *Geschwader*. His time on the triplane would be brief, however. Von Tutschek fell in combat on 15 March (six days before Operation *Michael* was scheduled), and a desperate call went out for a new *Kommandeur*.

A splendid example of a *Jasta* 18 Pfalz D IIIa in the famous 'Berthold colours' of dark blue fuselage and tail with a red nose is seen here. The pilot is Uffz Max Hitschler, posing at left with his groundcrew. The dark blue *Staffel* colour was applied to the uppersurfaces of the fuselage, tail and apparently both wings as well. The red nose display began just at the attachment point for the rear cabane strut. Hitschler's personal emblem consisted of the five vertical white stripes. This machine is something of a hybrid, as it is a D IIIa, but has the pointed lower wingtips generally associated with the D III. Hitschler left this machine behind when he followed his fellow *Jasta* 18 pilot Paul Strähle to the new *Jasta* 57 on 28 January 1918. It was then seemingly taken over by Ltn Hans Burkhard von Buttlar, who eventually had the white stripes painted over and an insignia of a hunting horn added in their place

A portion of a line-up of *Jasta* 15 (formerly *Jasta* 18) aircraft on Balatre airfield in early April 1918 shows two Pfalz D IIIa amidst the Albatros D V machines. Out of view is a third Pfalz D IIIa in Berthold's markings, which was at the far right end of this row of colourful machines. The Pfalz at left displays a white six-pointed star emblem, and had the uppersurfaces of both wings painted dark blue like the fuselage. The D IIIa at the extreme right boasted von Buttlar's horn emblem, and is believed to be the same D IIIa photographed with Hitschler at *Jasta* 18. The Albatros second from left still bears the white diamond band of Arthur Rahn, who by this time has transferred to *Jasta* 19 within JG II. It also apparently had the upper wing surfaces painted dark blue (*Arthur Rahn Collection, United States Air Force Museum*)

Following the swap of personnel between *Jagdstaffeln* 15 and 18 in March 1918, Ltn d R Hans Müller flew this Pfalz D IIIa bearing the famous '*Staffel Raben*' red and white colours and black raven insignia. His machine obviously suffered some major combat damage, and a relieved Müller poses for the obligatory photo after landing the aircraft safely. It is possible the D IIIa sustained a hit by flak, or maybe suffered a malfunction of the machine gun synchronisation system, which could splinter the propeller and cause major engine vibration. The *Staffel* marking of a red nose was extended back to the cockpit and a red border was applied to the cockpit rim. Uppersurfaces of both wings were also vermilion red, and a *Balkenkreuz* insignia is just discernible beneath the lower wing

The vacancy was filled when the renowned Hptm Rudolf Berthold brought his aggressive and demanding presence to the *Geschwader*. Still in recovery from his latest round of crippling wounds, he had previously commanded *Jasta* 18, where he had built up a 'sworn band' of proficient hunters. A few D III and D IIIa fighters already bore the red and blue colours of *Staffel* 18. Berthold ardently desired that the loyal pilots from his previous command come with him to JG II, and he proceeded to pull off an unprecedented stunt.

On 20 March he audaciously engineered a 'swap' of the entire pilot roster of *Jasta* 18 with *Jasta* 15 in JG II. This renumbering process took place at Guise in the 18. *Armee*. Berthold's men of the old *Jasta* 18 brought their Albatros and Pfalz to JG II and became the 'new' *Jasta* 15. Their counterparts in the old *Jasta* 15, now commanded by Ltn d R August Raben, relinquished their few Dr Is and left JG II for Bruille, in the 17. *Armee*, to become *Jasta* 18. Thus Berthold was able to begin the March offensive with his trusted band of eagles intact.

The Pfalz and Albatros of the 'new' *Jasta* 15 were photographed lined up on the JG II field at Balatre in early April 1918. Prominent at the head of the line-up is a Pfalz D IIIa resplendent in the famous red and dark blue heraldry of the 'Berthold' *Staffel*, and bearing the commander's equally renowned winged sword emblem. The question of how much Berthold actually flew this machine in combat is problematical. He had sustained a devastating wound to his upper right arm on 10 October 1917, eight days after his 28th victory, and even after his return to *Jasta* 18 the following March he was in terrible pain and unfit to fly. According to JG II historian Hanns Möller, Berthold did not fly again until 28 May, when he had acquired a new D VII.

Jasta 18, meanwhile, had relocated from the 17. *Armee* north to the 6. *Armee* as the offensive progressed. By mid-April the *Staffel* had settled in at Fachez, near Lille. The unit's Albatros and a single Dr I soon displayed the beautiful red noses, wings and white fuselages of the 'Raben' *Staffel*. At least one D IIIa also boasted these markings, along with the famous black raven emblem – the machine of Hans Müller, who survived the war with 12 victories (most scored in a D VII).

COLOUR PLATES

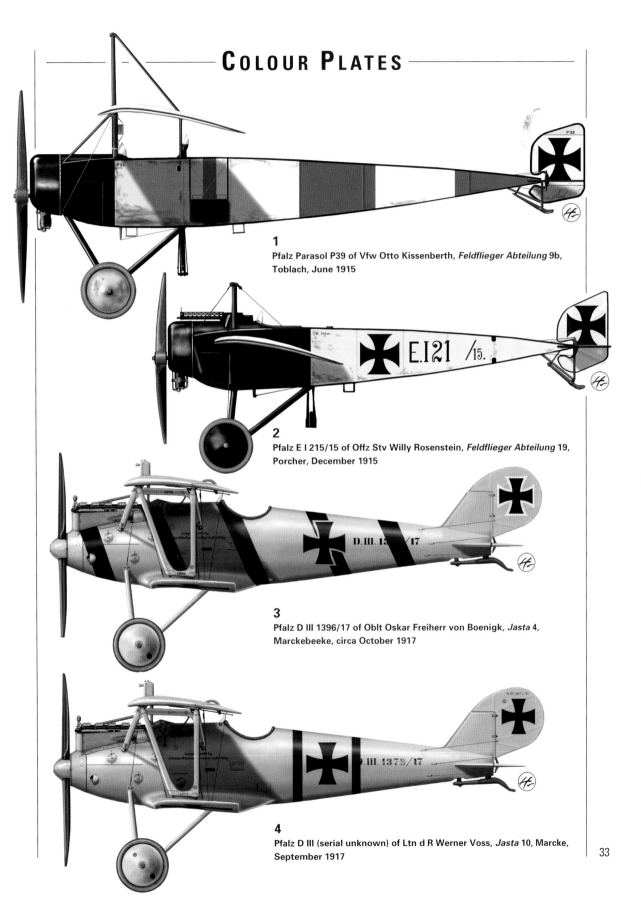

1
Pfalz Parasol P39 of Vfw Otto Kissenberth, *Feldflieger Abteilung* 9b, Toblach, June 1915

2
Pfalz E I 215/15 of Offz Stv Willy Rosenstein, *Feldflieger Abteilung* 19, Porcher, December 1915

3
Pfalz D III 1396/17 of Oblt Oskar Freiherr von Boenigk, *Jasta* 4, Marckebeeke, circa October 1917

4
Pfalz D III (serial unknown) of Ltn d R Werner Voss, *Jasta* 10, Marcke, September 1917

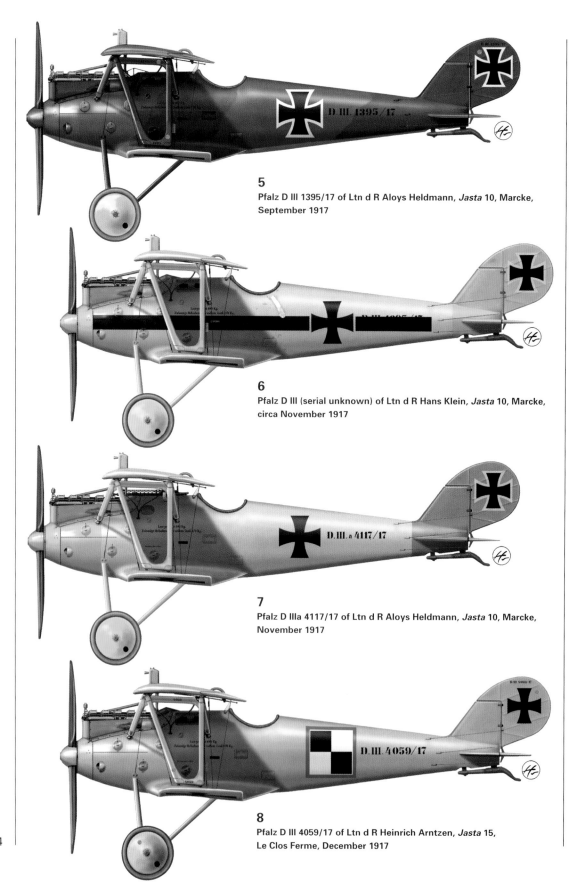

5
Pfalz D III 1395/17 of Ltn d R Aloys Heldmann, *Jasta* 10, Marcke, September 1917

6
Pfalz D III (serial unknown) of Ltn d R Hans Klein, *Jasta* 10, Marcke, circa November 1917

7
Pfalz D IIIa 4117/17 of Ltn d R Aloys Heldmann, *Jasta* 10, Marcke, November 1917

8
Pfalz D III 4059/17 of Ltn d R Heinrich Arntzen, *Jasta* 15, Le Clos Ferme, December 1917

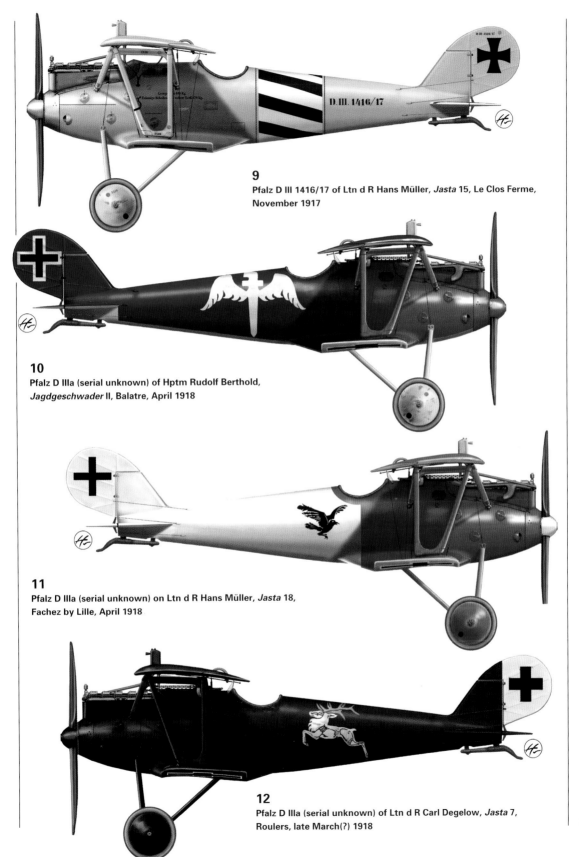

9
Pfalz D III 1416/17 of Ltn d R Hans Müller, *Jasta* 15, Le Clos Ferme,
November 1917

10
Pfalz D IIIa (serial unknown) of Hptm Rudolf Berthold,
Jagdgeschwader II, Balatre, April 1918

11
Pfalz D IIIa (serial unknown) on Ltn d R Hans Müller, *Jasta* 18,
Fachez by Lille, April 1918

12
Pfalz D IIIa (serial unknown) of Ltn d R Carl Degelow, *Jasta* 7,
Roulers, late March(?) 1918

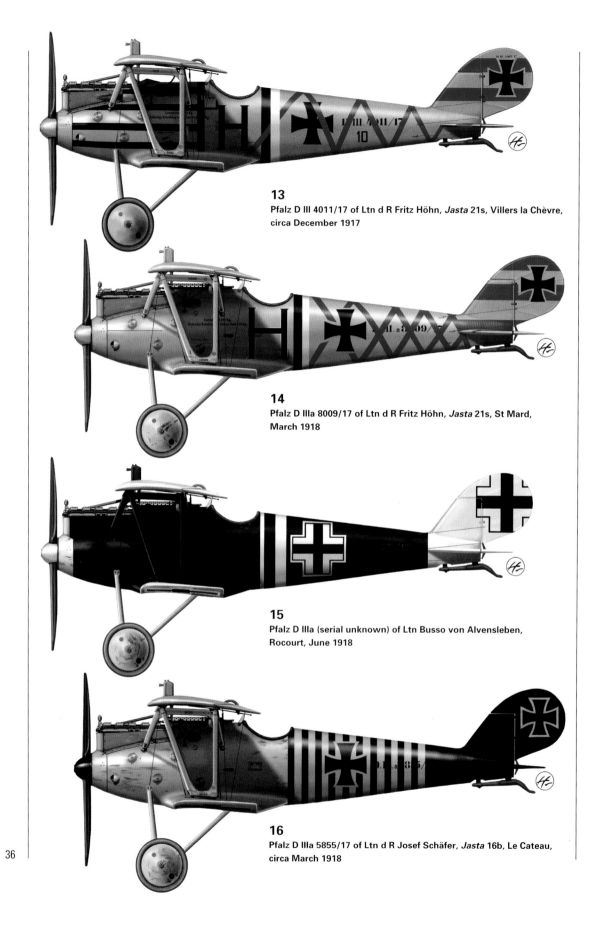

13
Pfalz D III 4011/17 of Ltn d R Fritz Höhn, *Jasta* 21s, Villers la Chèvre, circa December 1917

14
Pfalz D IIIa 8009/17 of Ltn d R Fritz Höhn, *Jasta* 21s, St Mard, March 1918

15
Pfalz D IIIa (serial unknown) of Ltn Busso von Alvensleben, Rocourt, June 1918

16
Pfalz D IIIa 5855/17 of Ltn d R Josef Schäfer, *Jasta* 16b, Le Cateau, circa March 1918

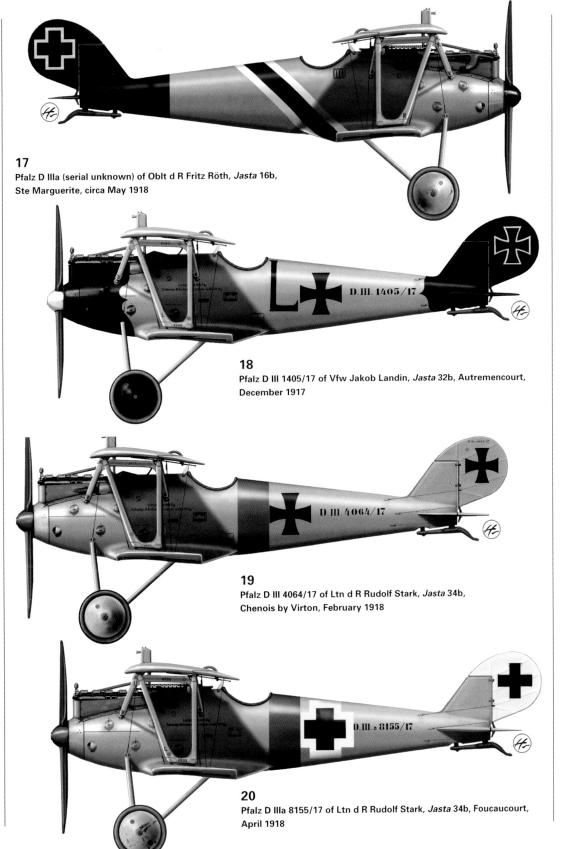

17
Pfalz D IIIa (serial unknown) of Oblt d R Fritz Röth, *Jasta* 16b,
Ste Marguerite, circa May 1918

18
Pfalz D III 1405/17 of Vfw Jakob Landin, *Jasta* 32b, Autremencourt,
December 1917

19
Pfalz D III 4064/17 of Ltn d R Rudolf Stark, *Jasta* 34b,
Chenois by Virton, February 1918

20
Pfalz D IIIa 8155/17 of Ltn d R Rudolf Stark, *Jasta* 34b, Foucaucourt,
April 1918

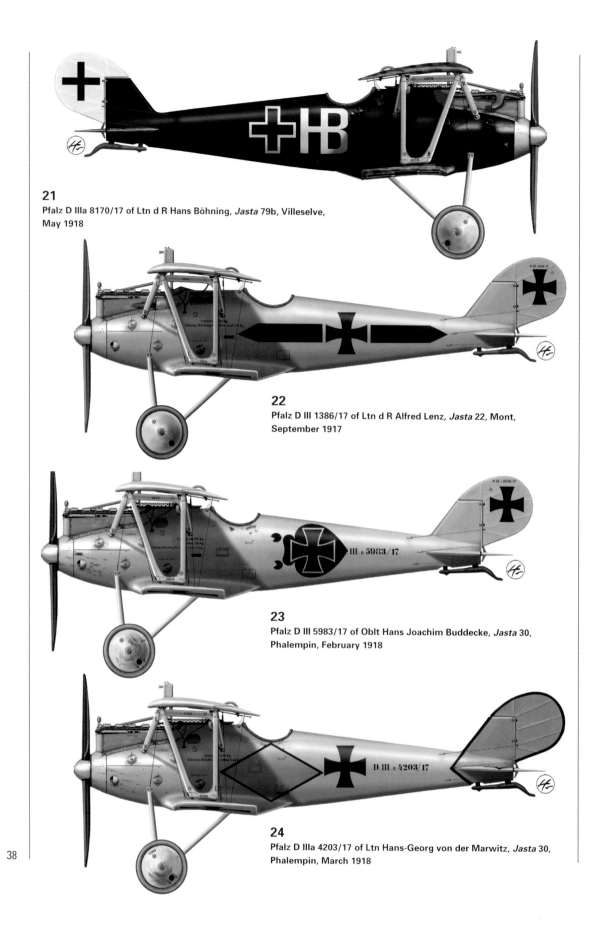

21
Pfalz D IIIa 8170/17 of Ltn d R Hans Böhning, *Jasta* 79b, Villeselve,
May 1918

22
Pfalz D III 1386/17 of Ltn d R Alfred Lenz, *Jasta* 22, Mont,
September 1917

23
Pfalz D III 5983/17 of Oblt Hans Joachim Buddecke, *Jasta* 30,
Phalempin, February 1918

24
Pfalz D IIIa 4203/17 of Ltn Hans-Georg von der Marwitz, *Jasta* 30,
Phalempin, March 1918

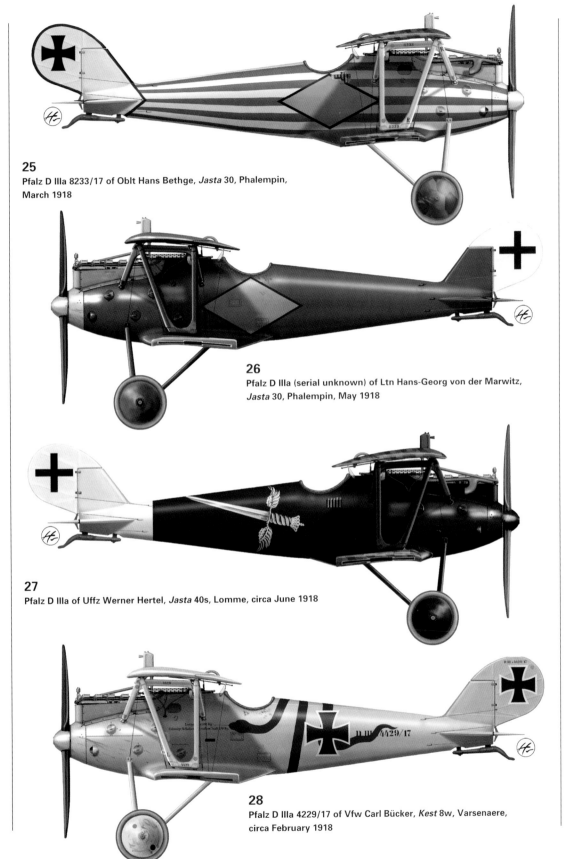

25
Pfalz D IIIa 8233/17 of Oblt Hans Bethge, *Jasta* 30, Phalempin,
March 1918

26
Pfalz D IIIa (serial unknown) of Ltn Hans-Georg von der Marwitz,
Jasta 30, Phalempin, May 1918

27
Pfalz D IIIa of Uffz Werner Hertel, *Jasta* 40s, Lomme, circa June 1918

28
Pfalz D IIIa 4229/17 of Vfw Carl Bücker, *Kest* 8w, Varsenaere,
circa February 1918

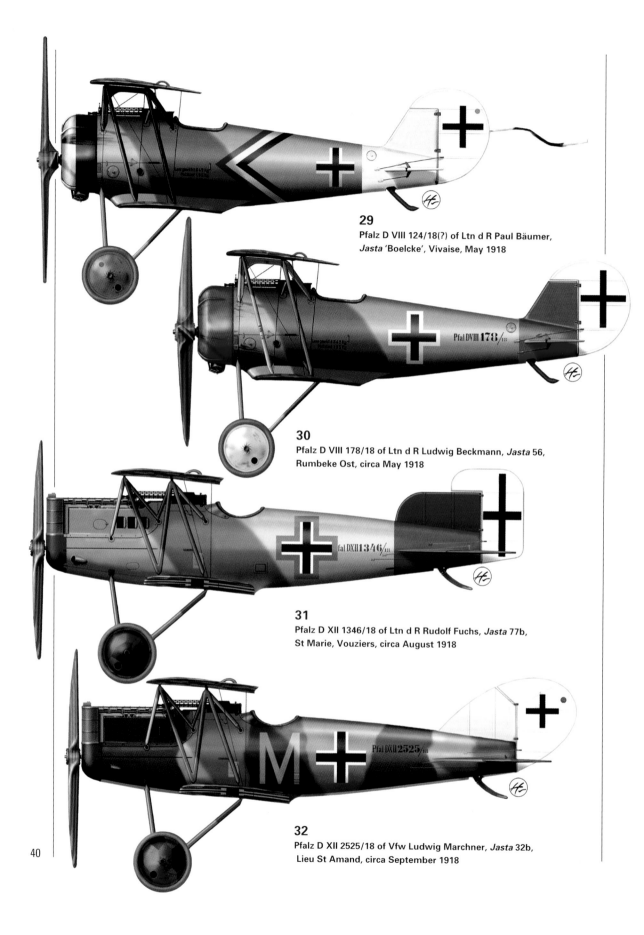

29
Pfalz D VIII 124/18(?) of Ltn d R Paul Bäumer,
Jasta 'Boelcke', Vivaise, May 1918

30
Pfalz D VIII 178/18 of Ltn d R Ludwig Beckmann, *Jasta* 56,
Rumbeke Ost, circa May 1918

31
Pfalz D XII 1346/18 of Ltn d R Rudolf Fuchs, *Jasta* 77b,
St Marie, Vouziers, circa August 1918

32
Pfalz D XII 2525/18 of Vfw Ludwig Marchner, *Jasta* 32b,
Lieu St Amand, circa September 1918

Profile 1

Profile 15

41

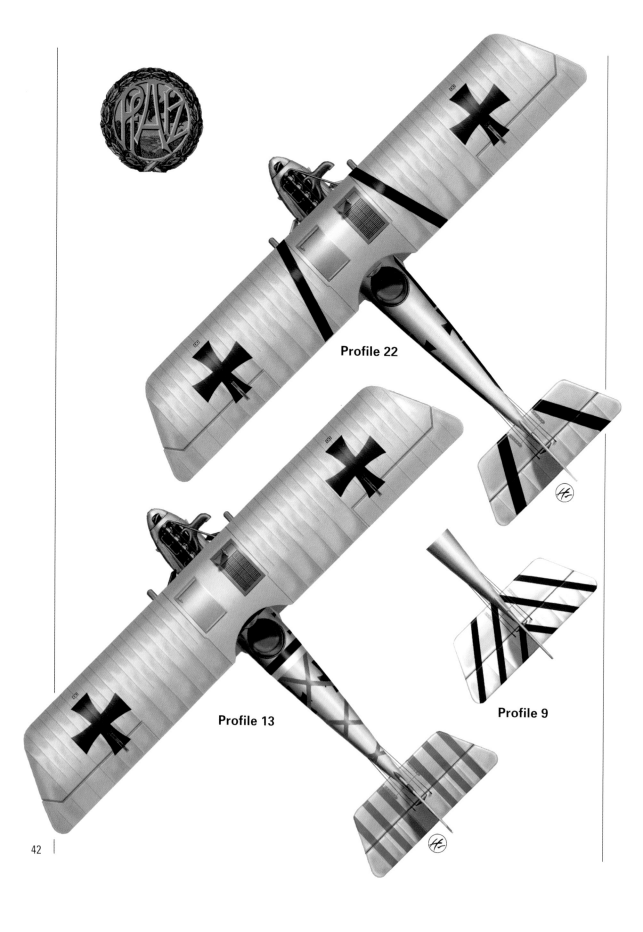

Profile 22

Profile 13

Profile 9

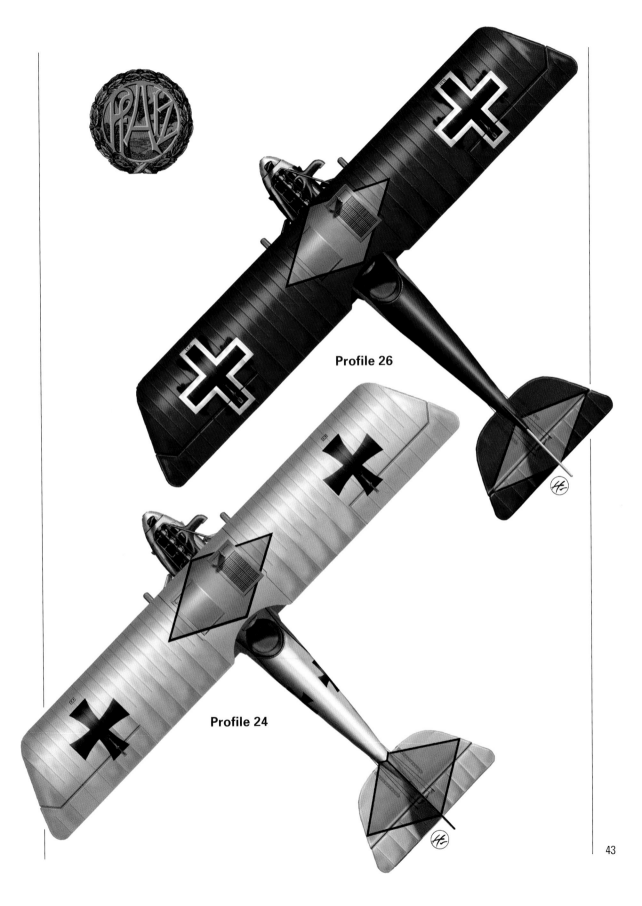

Profile 26

Profile 24

43

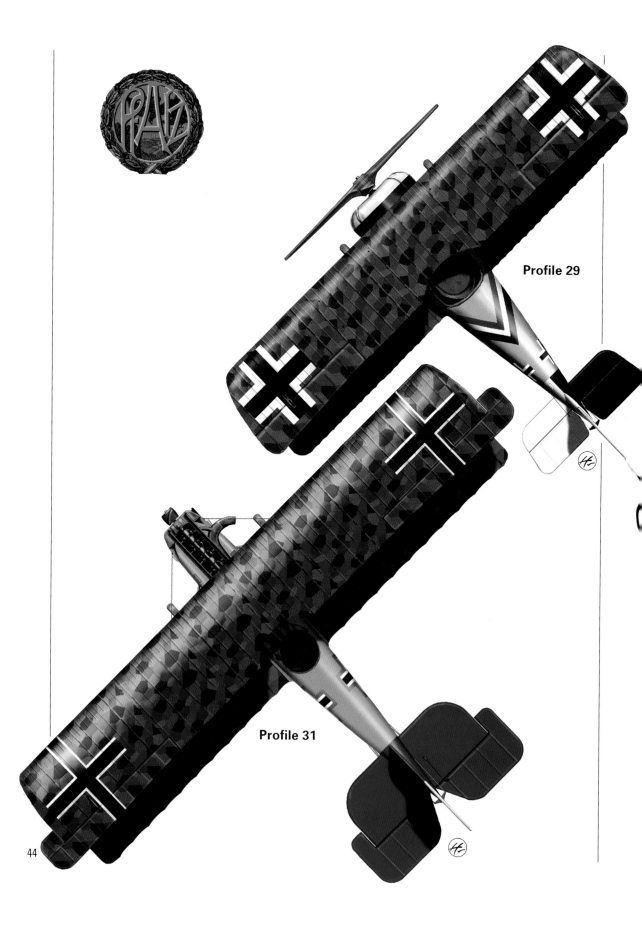

Profile 29

Profile 31

HOME-GROWN BAVARIAN FIGHTER

The Kingdom of Bavaria was the second most powerful state in Imperial Germany after Prussia. Even as part of the second German Reich, Bavaria retained considerable military privileges. It established its own training and reconnaissance formations, and by 1917 the move was made to establish Bavarian fighter units. On 17 July 1917 the existing *Jagdstaffeln* 16, 23, 32, 34 and 35 were converted to Bavarian units, although the transfers of Bavarian personnel into these squadrons to replace non-Bavarians who were posted out took some time. Later, five more *Staffeln* were created as Bavarian formations; *Jastas* 76 through 80.

As the Pfalz Flugzeugwerke in Speyer was a Bavarian enterprise, it would seem logical that many of these units were equipped either partially or entirely with the D III/D IIIa at one time. This chapter will examine some of the Bavarian units and pilots that flew the Pfalz in combat.

Jasta 16b

Jasta 16 was created from *KEK* Ensisheim, the early single-seater formation in which Otto Kissenberth first made a name as a fighter pilot. He left the unit in August 1917 shortly before the first Pfalz D IIIs began to arrive. Max Holtzem, whom we also met in Chapter One, managed to obtain a posting out of Bavarian *Flieger Schule* I and joined *Jasta* 16b in August 1917. He recalled that he was flying a Pfalz D III with the *Staffel* as early as September, when the unit was at Spincourt, on the Verdun front, in the 5. *Armee*. He wrote;

'*Jasta* 16b was never fully equipped with Pfalz D IIIs. But at Verdun I flew a zebra-striped Pfalz D III, fuselage black and white and tail all black. My symbol the comet was the guardian-angel who flew with me. It was my dear mother who I had lost when I was nine years old. It was on my Pfalz D III in 1917 at Verdun and in Flanders, 1918 at the Somme and later the Ypres offensives. It was elaborated very nicely in black and white over the silver colour on each side of the fuselage of my Pfalz.'

Uniquely, Holtzem recalled that the Pfalz D III was a delight to fly. 'You flew this little bird. It was a real pilot's aeroplane'. He remembered that its ability to spin beautifully to the left saved his life more than

Although blemished, this photograph affords a view of Vfw Max Holtzem of *Jasta* 16b with his familiar Pfalz D IIIa. Holtzem's personal emblem was the black and white comet applied over a field of black stripes. The black tail unit marking is seen, as well as the commonly applied black spinners on the Pfalz in the background. Although the lower starboard wing appears darker than the silver grey fuselage, it is the author's opinion that this is due to a common optical effect. The eight-pointed star at the head of the comet was also applied to the port upper wing in some form

once. He felt that the Pfalz could outdive many contemporary aircraft, and the type did indeed have a reputation as a superb diver. With full power, Holtzem remembered, the pilot had to keep slight forward stick pressure, as the aircraft tried to go into a slight climb. With the power off it became nose-heavy and fell off to the right in a shallow dive. Holtzem insisted that the Pfalz was in many ways superior to the Albatros, and was 'a great aeroplane on low level missions such as trench strafing and ground attack'. It was easy to land, and he often wheel-landed his Pfalz to save his tailskid from damage on the rough aerodromes of the day.

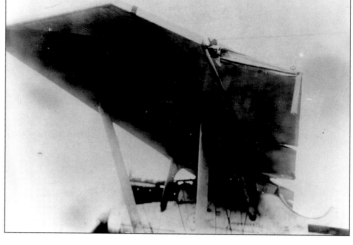

Holtzem recalled 13 December 1917;

'On this winter morning, three German machines had started to attack an observation balloon near Belleville. They were Vfw (Fritz) Schattauer and (Johann) Neumaier, flying Albatros D IIIs and myself in a Pfalz D III. While Schattauer, flying in centre position at 1500 metres altitude, plunged down at the captive balloon, the other two of us attacked the two Paul Schmitts who were attempting to come to the defence of the balloon.

'Vfw Neumaier attacked the nearest of the two-seaters from the rear and sent him down in flames with a short burst. The second aeroplane fled and I followed behind, but before I could fire at my opponent several Nieuports attacked me. In crossfire with the French, I was able, by skillful flying and manoeuvring, to defend myself for a brief period. However, my aeroplane was struck by a number of bursts, causing serious damage. Pretending to be out of control, I spun down. Soaked by fuel escaping from the reserve tank, I was almost blinded, and as I neared the ground I recovered control. The French, who had assumed that they had finished me off, fortunately did not follow me, so I was able to make a safe landing inside our lines, despite the shell-torn terrain.'

By January 1918, Holtzem was one of the most seasoned pilots in the *Jasta*. Nine of the twelve pilots under the command of Ltn Heinrich Geigl on 20 January had been posted to the unit since September, with little frontline experience – it is doubtful that they all held Holtzem's high opinion of the Pfalz. *Jasta* 16b was but one of several *Staffeln* that submitted complaints about worrisome deflection or bending of the upper wingtips of their Pfalz. The unit installed auxiliary bracing cables to reinforce the tips, and reported that without the cables the wings would have failed. A much more dangerous problem was experienced by Vfw Andreas Triebswetter on 20 January, who reported;

'On 20 January 1918, in aircraft Pfalz D III 4057, I made a combat patrol with a *Kette* of four aircraft. While diving, the outer tip of the left aileron broke. I was diving in a totally straight direction without banking. It cannot be assumed that the break can be traced back to the effects of enemy fire, because during the dive enemy flak occurred only weakly and quite far away from me.

On 20 January 1918 Vfw Andreas Triebswetter was making a straight dive in Pfalz D III 4057/17 when the outer 25 percent of the port aileron suddenly broke away. Triebswetter, who would eventually attain four victories, was able to make a safe landing and submit an account of the structural failure. This photograph was taken and submitted along with his report, and it shows that the entire balance portion of the aileron was gone. Note the black spinner and a portion of Triebswetter's personal insignia visible by the cockpit (*HAC/UTD*)

Another of the photographs submitted with the report on D III 4057/17, this one shows the outline of the missing aileron section traced in white ink. A similar incident happened to ace Heinrich Kroll of Saxon *Jasta* 24 on 25 January 1918 when the rear spar of his D IIIa broke and his port aileron was half torn off. Kroll skillfully managed to land his Pfalz (*HAC/UTD*)

Josef Schäfer of *Jasta* 16b peers at the camera from his D IIIa 5855/17. This aircraft bore a striking pattern of personal black stripes similar to those seen on Holtzem's Pfalz, extending from the unit's black tail up to the cockpit. It is likely that the machine had a black spinner as well. Note the flare cartridge rack mounted on the fuselage. Ltn d R Schäfer scored three victories in the *Staffel*, and he may have been flying a Pfalz for his first (an SE 5 downed on 12 June 1918). A Bristol fell to his guns on 2 July, then on 10 October he was credited with an RE 8 brought down at 1730 hrs west of Ypres. However, Schäfer himself died later that same day

It is just as unlikely that the break can be traced back to ground machine guns because I was crossing the enemy lines at a height of about 2000 metres.'

In addition, the deputy *Staffel-führer* wrote that the aileron lost about a quarter of its surface. The aircraft had only seen 21.5 hours of flight time to that point. The same Pfalz had a break in the upper fuselage longeron only days before, 'not as a result of immoderate stress during a bad landing'. Furthermore, a similar structural break in the outer wingtip had happened on D III 4040/17 just weeks before;

'Thus, these damages do not help to increase the pilots' trust in this product. When the tips of the lower wings are bent so sharply upwards in the air so that it almost looks dangerous from the ground, then the securing of the aileron is, at any rate, insufficient.'

On 27 January, the *Jasta* lost further faith in the Pfalz when the neophyte Uffz Eugen Förtig was killed in the crash of D III 4034/17 on Mercy-le-Haute airfield. On 7 February the *Staffel* completed a move to Aertrycke in the 4. *Armee* sector of Flanders. Two weeks later another Pfalz crash occurred, Uffz Rudolf Lingenfelder dying in D III 4062/17. Triebswetter, having survived his hair-raising aileron break, went on to torch a balloon on 8 March for his first of four victories.

Six days later the *Staffel* moved to Le Cateau, and thus on 18 March it was one of the several units that participated in the massive 'air battle of Le Cateau'. Ltn Geigl accounted for his seventh opponent that day, and Holtzem brought down the SE 5 of 2Lt H A Payne of No 84 Sqn, who landed intact behind the German lines. After returning to his airfield, Holtzem rushed out to the British fighter with some mechanics and flew the RFC scout back to his unit. Ironically, because there were no witnesses to his combat he failed to receive credit for this victory!

About two weeks later, Geigl flew his Albatros to lead a patrol through the fog. Holtzem recalled;

The ill-fated Uffz Rudolf Lingenfelder poses with his D III 4062/17 of *Jasta* 16b. The black tail was the unit marking of this *Staffel*, and the colour was generally applied to the propeller spinner as well. Lingenfelder's career was tragically brief, and typical of the group of replacement pilots the *Staffel* received in December 1917. Lingenfelder arrived on 9 December, and on 21 February 1918 he crashed to his death on Aertrycke airfield in this D III

A group of Pfalz D IIIa fighters of *Jasta* 16b show off their black tails and spinners. The third aircraft from right boasts lengthwise black stripes as a personal marking. Although Max Holtzem stated that Bavarian *Jagdstaffel* 16 never had a full complement of Pfalz, the unit had a good number of D IIIa machines on hand nevertheless (*J Young*)

Although not fully documented, this retouched photograph is believed to *possibly* show the *Jasta* 16b *Staffelführer* Fritz Röth in a Pfalz D IIIa. It is known that Röth flew Albatros machines for his victories prior to obtaining a Fokker D VII, but he certainly had opportunity to fly the Pfalz in *Jasta* 16b. The black and white fuselage sash would have made a distinctive individual marking, although the lack of a fuselage cross is puzzling. Presumably, the cross was painted over in silver-grey paint, probably so that it would not conflict with the personal emblem. If this is indeed a *Jasta* 16b machine, it would have had the usual black tail and spinner. Röth was characterised by his comrades as a modest idealist, and deeply religious. After the Armistice he returned to his hometown of Nürnberg, depressed by the defeat and revolution in his homeland and reportedly troubled by the lives he had taken in combat. Röth committed suicide on New Year's Eve 1918

'It was on 4 April 1918 that I could have died instead of Geigl when, over the Somme, leading under the misty fog because I didn't want to collide, a Camel spotted me and dove down shooting. I was alert, made one spinning turn and saw Geigl and the Camel colliding in fire.'

Both Geigl and the Camel pilot from No 65 Sqn fell to their deaths near Warfusée.

Geigl's successor as *Staffel* commander was Oblt Fritz Röth, the veteran balloon-buster from *Jasta* 23b. Vfw Hans Schorn was posted to the *Staffel* at about the same time as Röth, but his time at the front would be brief. On 21 May Schorn was flying in a *Kette* of six Pfalz which had the extreme misfortune of meeting Capt Edward 'Mick' Mannock and a patrol of No 74 Sqn SE 5as. Mannock claimed one Pfalz 'shot to pieces after firing

a long burst from directly behind and above', and two more out of control. The first was certainly Schorn, but the *Staffel* lost no other pilots.

Röth did not claim any victims for some time after his arrival. On 29 May, flying an Albatros, he attacked a British line of ten balloons and 'roasted' five of them in one incredible sortie. By the time he claimed again – a Bristol on 25 July for his 16th of 28 eventual successes – the *Staffel* had apparently turned in its Pfalz for Fokker D VIIs.

Jasta 32b

Jasta 32b received its first examples of the Pfalz in the winter of 1917/18. The unit was based at Autremencourt in the 7. *Armee*, and was commanded by the famed Bavarian ace Oblt Eduard Schleich. This *Jasta* does not seem to have had a large number of Pfalz, and remained primarily an Albatros *Staffel*.

One pilot who flew a Pfalz during his brief career in *Jasta* 32b was Vfw Jakob Landin. Born on 21 August 1892 in Westheim, Landin had previously flown in Bavarian Fl. Abt. 295(A) before arriving at the *Staffel* on 8 December 1917. Landin needed little time to kick off his career as a fighter pilot – only 15 days later he was credited with a Paul Schmitt two-seater near Vailly-sur-Aisne for his first (and the unit's 19th) *Luftsieg*. He quickly followed this up with a Nieuport over Paissy on 6 January 1918. This was probably Nieuport 24 N5449, flown by MdL Henri Durand of *Escadrille* N89, who was taken PoW. He had been attacking a balloon when he suffered engine trouble, then was seemingly attacked by Landin.

On 10 January the *Staffel* was relocated to Mars-sour-Bourcq in the 3. *Armee*. Eleven days later, a Pfalz was once again an engine of tragedy for a novice *Jagdflieger*.

Nineteen-year-old Gefr Josef Mayer was killed in a D IIIa during a practice flight, the wing breaking off the Pfalz fighter at a height of 800 metres and the machine subsequently crashing on the *Staffel* airfield.

Pfalz D IIIa 1346/18 is seen between two Albatros D Va machines of *Jagdstaffel* 16b, providing evidence that the *Staffel* did indeed operate a mixed bag of equipment. All three fighters display black tails and spinners, and the two Albatros scouts show off personal fuselage markings as well. Aircraft 1346/18 came from the very last D IIIa batch (serials 1250 to 1349/18), which was ordered in February 1918 (*J Young*)

This D III 1405/17 is a splendid example of a *Jasta* 32b Pfalz. Flown by Vfw Jakob Landin, the aircraft featured a black tail, white spinner and black nose trim – markings that are believed to have been standard within the *Staffel*, although Landin's machine displayed a stylish scalloped application of the nose and tail colours. The black 'L' was an obvious choice of individual badge for Landin, whose proud groundcrew poses with their charge. Note the circular Pfalz logo, serial number and 'R' stencilling on the starboard (right) interplane and cabane struts (*HAC/UTD*)

This time Jakob Landin himself appears in the cockpit of his elegantly decorated fighter. The scalloped nose and tail markings and the black wheel covers are all in evidence. Landin attained three victories before his death on 27 February 1918. He had returned early from a patrol due to engine trouble, only to perish in a fiery crash of his aircraft on Guesnain aerodrome (*HAC/UTD*)

On 14 February the *Jasta* was transferred to Guesnain, near Douai, in the 17. *Armee*. Thus Landin could add a British aircraft to his tally on 23 February, when he was credited with an RE 8 at 1535 hrs near Willerval – another RE 8 was also confirmed to Ltn d R Fritz Danker for his second victory. Landin's joy over his rising score would be short-lived, however. Four days later he took off at 1700 hrs with four companions. Thirty minutes later he returned to Guesnain, apparently suffering mechanical trouble. In front of the horrified eyes of his comrades, Landin plunged to the airfield from 150 metres and died in a fiery crash.

On 17 April Ltn d R Danker was badly injured during a test flight in D IIIa 8269/17 when it crashed on Guesnain field – he died on the 23rd.

By the end of May the *Staffel* had begun to receive Roland D VIa machines to replace its weary Albatros and Pfalz fighters.

Jasta 34b

This unit was formed at FEA 1 at Altenburg on 20 February 1917. By the time it was assigned its first Pfalz D IIIs in September 1917, the unit had achieved 23 victories flying entirely on the French front. Based at Mont, near Verdun, since 5 September, the *Jasta* was commanded by Oblt Robert Greim. Born in Bayreuth on 22 June 1892, Greim was a career army officer who had by then garnered five of his eventual 28 victories. Greim test-flew Pfalz D III 1385/17 on 11 September and was not impressed, his flight log reading;

'Machine in every respect inferior to the Albatros D V. Very heavy control forces, very nose heavy, very slow, inferior rate of climb – 4000 metres in 35-36 minutes.'

In spite of Greim's glum assessment, *Jasta* 34b continued to receive both the D III and D IIIa. However, Greim and many of his experienced pilots continued to fly the Albatros too. The luckless *Staffel* achieved but three victories from October through December for the loss of three pilots killed, two taken PoW and another wounded. Things brightened in the New Year as four French aircraft were destroyed in the first three days of 1918. On the 9th, however, D III 4031/17 took 40 hits from flak shrapnel and Ltn Hans Kiessling was badly wounded in the left thigh.

Rudolf Stark's first fighter was Pfalz D III 4064/17, here probably photographed at Chenois aerodrome. Stark's personal emblem of a lilac fuselage band and spinner adorned all of his various Pfalz aircraft. In this case it was somewhat roughly applied, and just slightly overlapped the horizontal arm of the national insignia. The fuselage exhibits signs of hard use and the harmful effects of storing machines in unheated hangars and damp field conditions. In some cases the fuselages became so warped due to moisture absorption that the flying characteristics were compromised (*A Imrie*)

Nine days later a replacement pilot arrived on the airfield at Chenois – Ltn d R Rudolf Stark. This airman was a gifted artist and writer who would leave an impressive record in paintings, photos and in his evocative book *Die Jagdstaffel unsere Heimat* (English title, *Wings of War*).

Born on 11 February 1897 at Neuburg, on the Danube, Stark volunteered for the 2nd Bavarian Uhlan Regiment and would serve in France, Poland and the Ukraine. He received the Bavarian Military Merit Order 4th Class with Swords on 29 September 1915, as well as the Iron Cross 2nd Class. Stark applied for transfer to the air service in 1917, and following flight training was posted to Bavarian Fl. Abt. 296(A) on 15 November. He took fighter training at *Jastaschule* II and arrived at *Jasta* 34b on 18 January 1918, thrilled to finally be a *Jagdflieger*;

'My first visit is to the new machine. A Pfalz D III stands silver-like in the hangar. I stroke the cockpit and play on the bracing wires that sing like violin strings. My identification markings are painted on the machine – a lilac stripe behind the cockpit and a lilac coat for the propeller spinner.

'Three of us fly to the front. There is not much to do – we are the only aircraft to be seen far and wide. The old, familiar countryside glides away beneath me. The sun gleams on my wings. Often I stroke the machine parts about me and pat the silver skin of my aircraft, just as I used to pat my horse.'

Such carefree musings came to an abrupt end a few days later. During a 'joyous onslaught' on a Caudron, Stark was jumped by a French fighter;

'I go into a turn at once, but my opponent is sitting on my neck all the time, and soon his bullets hit my machine. A violent blow on my shoulder pushes me down in my seat, and for a brief space my machine goes into a spin. I catch it again, but the rattling continues behind me as I go into turn after turn. Petrol squirts out round my legs, and my petrol gauge tells me I have lost a lot of juice.'

Stark flew northward in zigzags, hoping to reach his lines before his fuel gave out. Confused and concerned by the occasional rattling from behind, and dizzy from his frantic stunting, he could see no Frenchman behind him. He reached his aerodrome on empty tanks. Stark looked over his D III 4064/17 and counted 16 holes, two in the main tank. He was chagrined to discover that his shoulder strap had been shot through

Stark strikes a rather melodramatic pose with his later Pfalz D IIIa 8155/17, circa April 1918. This machine had a flare cartridge rack affixed to the starboard fuselage side. Just aft of Stark's usual lilac fuselage band is an early form of *Balkenkreuz* insignia, affected by using the widest part of the previous iron cross as the *Balken* or bar width. This produced a cross with bars of a ratio (width to length) of 1:3 at best – also note the extremely thick white borders. It was soon realised that this form of insignia was difficult to recognise as a cross at any distance and it was quickly altered (*A Imrie*)

and one end had hung loose in the slipstream – the 'rattle' which had worried him was the strap buckle banging against the fuselage!

On 16 March the *Staffel* relocated to Le Cateau airfield opposite the British in preparation for the great Spring Offensive. The pilots shared Le Cateau with their fellow Bavarians of *Jasta* 16b – both were components of *Jagdgruppe* 10 under Greim. On 21 March *Kaiserschlacht* erupted, and the *Staffel* braved the thick mist to down two opponents. Two days later Stark achieved his first victory when he stumbled onto two DH 4s in the thick smoke over Péronne. He would later admit this victory was a fluke. With a sputtering engine and jammed guns, Stark bore down on one of the big bombers when suddenly his guns cleared and he sent a telling burst into the de Havilland.

On 24 March the *Staffel* started its patrol into the crowded skies over the battle raging near Péronne. They spotted an approaching formation that materialised into Camels. Stark would write;

'Now those machines are above us, and we spot their cockades in the sunshine. We close up and await their attack. A signal flare shines out on high and sinks toward us with long trails of smoke – the sign to attack, given by the English leader. They dive down on us, and already they are in our midst.

'Turn, turn, turn, high and low. Tracer bullets cleave the air. Machine guns rattle everywhere, engines roar, bracing wires groan and howl in dives. I see a Sopwith attack the Albatros in front of me and take a deflection shot at him. He breaks away and goes into a turn to escape. Our turns grow narrower and narrower, my sights follow his fuselage, and it looks as if my machine guns were joined onto his tail. My tracer bullets skim along the edge of his fuselage, but again and again he pulls himself out of my sights.

'At last I get on the mark – a hit. Fuel squirts out of the machine and hangs in a long streamer of haze from its tail. The Englishman is hit and goes down in a spin. I have no time to follow him down because I am attacked at once.'

The Camel went down to crash-land west of Barleux in the British lines. Later, the same patrol engaged a flight of No 56 Sqn SE 5as and destroyed two of them – a gratifying day for the *Staffel*.

On the afternoon of 30 March, the *Jasta* once again endured the worsening weather to support the field grey troops as they attacked Hamelet. They took a hand in the battle raging on the ground by strafing British trenches and artillery positions. Stark wrote;

'Now English fighting machines make their appearance. They flit like shadows through the shreds of clouds and try to attack our infantry. They are not going to succeed because we are there, so they wheel about and turn off.

'The rain becomes thicker – it whips against the skin like hail. Goggles are continually dimmed, but carry on! A Sopwith hurtles out of a cloud in front of me. He sees me and goes into a turn, but for a moment he

Stark stares at the camera as a groundcrewman helps him fasten his safety straps in the cockpit of what is believed to be D IIIa 8155/17. The lilac stripe is clearly seen. Regarding the finish of the Pfalz fighters he knew so well, Stark later wrote, 'All Pfalz D III and D IIIa were delivered in a silver paint finish. The various *Staffel* and pilot markings were painted over this at the individual *Staffeln*, where half of the fuselage was often coloured but silver always remained typical for the Pfalz' (*A Imrie*)

An atmospheric scene is presented as Stark, at right, prepares for a flight in another one of his D IIIa fighters as the engine is run up. This aircraft is thought to be D IIIa 8178/17, which displayed the later, more correct, style of *Balkenkreuz* insignia (*A Imrie*)

stands quite still in the middle of it. I take aim – shoot – my tracers hiss across to him in long threads and eat their way into his fuselage. A red flame jets out, and wing over wing the Englishman goes down in flames – my third!'

Stark's victim was Sopwith Dolphin C3791 of No 79 Sqn, its pilot, 2Lt H Browne, being taken PoW east of Vaire.

On 4 April Ludendorff launched his final modest assault of *Kaiserschlacht*, attempting to gain a foothold between Hamel and Grivesnes. *Jasta* 34b took off at 1445 hrs in pelting rain to support the infantry. The mist and clouds were so thick collisions were narrowly avoided. Stark surprised an RE 8 before the observer could use his Lewis gun, sending it down to crash near Fouilloy. The *Staffel* landed at 1630 hrs, but desperate appeals for help from the harried infantry necessitated another sortie in a torrential downpour. Stark shot down a DH 4 in flames south of Hamlet to 'make ace'.

According to the *Staffel* war diary, the unit received the first examples of the D IIIa on 10 April. Eight days later the *Jasta* took up new quarters at Foucaucourt, where it was soon joined by *Jagdstaffeln* 37 and 77b in *Jagdgruppe* 'Greim'. In the late afternoon of 25 April a patrol was bounced by two SE 5a flights from No 84 Sqn. Capt J V Sorsoleil reported;

'While on patrol we dived on a large formation of silver-coloured Pfalz and Albatros V-strutters. I observed one of our machines fighting two Pfalz. I dived on the nearest and fired a long burst with both guns. He went down vertically and a big cloud of smoke emerged from his engine.'

After the mêlée, the RAF pilots were credited with seven opponents downed – *Jasta* 34b actually lost Uffz August Meyer killed (probably by Sorsoleil) and Oblt Dieterle was wounded, but landed safely behind German lines. The *Staffel* war diary records the pilots' depression over the obvious inferiority of their aircraft this day.

In late May a few cast-off Fokker Dr Is from JG I were acquired, but most of the *Staffel* operations continued on the old Pfalz biplanes. On 19 May the unit achieved a notable success when it took part in bringing down three Bristols from No 62 Sqn in German territory. Stark and Vfw Max Kahlow forced F 2B C4751 to land near Proyart. There were no shared victories in the *Jagdstaffeln*, so Kahlow got the credit for this victory – his fifth. However, in the same scrap Ltn Karl Bauernfeind's D IIIa 8023/17 had taken a number of crippling hits, and the pilot suffered a skull fracture in the ensuing crash-landing.

On 24 May Stark was named acting commander of *Jasta* 77b and left the *Staffel*. With a total of five victories scored on the D III and D IIIa, Stark qualifies as a true Pfalz ace. Be that as it may, on 28 May the *Jasta* war diary bitterly reported, 'The unit had daily sorties and combats, but with its old and worn-out machines, it had become weak and powerless'.

This situation would not be remedied until 15 June when the unit's first Fokker D VIIs arrived.

Jasta 35b

The first Pfalz D IIIs were issued to *Jasta* 35b on 3 November 1917, but the unit was never fully equipped with the type. In fact, the story of the Pfalz in *Jasta* 35b is largely a tale of woe. Even so, the Pfalz *Flugzeugwerke* was mindful of its image among its customers, and the *Staffel* war diary

On 25 April 1918, Flg Andreas Köhler of *Jasta* 35b was on a practice flight in D IIIa 8282/17 when he was wounded by flak and brought down near Vimy-Combles, behind the British lines. His Pfalz fell in to British hands largely intact and was given the number 'G/3Bde/4'. This photograph was taken the next day at No 2 Aircraft Depot at Candas as Capt C E Williamson-Jones of No 9 Sqn inspected the machine guns of 8282/17. It may be noted that a start has been made towards altering the fuselage cross to *Balkenkreuz* format. The report on this machine stated that the wings were covered with printed 'lozenge' camouflage fabric (many Pfalz in this late production batch had five-colour fabric on the wings), and that they still had the iron cross form of insignia

Gefr Jakob Tischner of *Jasta* 35b managed to damage not one but two of his unit's aircraft on 17 June 1918. He was landing in the new Roland D VIa 1205/18 (in the foreground) and rolled into a collision with Pfalz D IIIa 8132/17 in the background. This view of the Pfalz shows the *Staffel* marking of a white chevron on the upper wing, and an early style of *Balkenkreuz* insignia. Just visible are two or three black(?) stripes on the fuselage aft of the cross, which were the unknown pilot's insignia. The change to *Balkenkreuz* had not yet been effected on the Roland D VIa (*A Imrie*)

records that the unit's Christmas Eve party of 1917 was made all the merrier by lavish amounts of food and drink supplied by the Pfalz firm (not to be outdone, but a trifle late, the Fokker company sent four crates of Christmas packages which arrived on 10 January 1918).

In early February 1918 the *Jasta* prepared to move from Premont to Emerchicourt. On the 10th, Ltn d R Robert Denkhardt crashed fatally in D IIIa 4163/17 as he was leaving Premont. The hard-pressed *Jasta* suffered more setbacks in the next two months, and on 25 April Flg Andreas Köhler was wounded and taken PoW during a practice flight in D IIIa 8282/17.

On 13 June, Rudolf Stark was transferred from acting command of *Jasta* 77b to full leadership of *Jasta* 35b. Upon his arrival at Epinoy, Stark recorded, 'Things do not look too good in this *Staffel*. Three leaders have fallen within a brief space of time. Our machines are old Albatros D Vs and Pfalz D IIIs, without much fighting value'.

Some newer Roland D VIa machines were also on hand, but on 17 June Gefr Tischner crashed his Roland into Pfalz D IIIa 8132/17 while landing and damaged both aircraft. Finally, on 1 July 1918 Stark led a

sortie into cloudy skies, and despite poor visibility, found an artillery-spotting RE 8 and shot it down northwest of Arras – the first victory for the unit in over two months. *Jasta* 35b happily exchanged an Albatros, two Pfalz and three Rolands for six Fokker D VIIs on 24 August.

Jasta 79b

This unit was formed at FEA 1b, Schleissheim, between 8 November 1917 and 2 February 1918, and was equipped entirely with the Pfalz D III and D IIIa. The first commander was Ltn d R Xaver Dannhüber, who had scored ten victories in *Jasta* 26. He was wounded on 18 October 1917, and after his recovery was posted briefly to *Jasta* 76b before being placed in command of 79b. On 2 February the *Staffel* was transferred to an aerodrome at Thugny, near Rethel (in the 3. *Armee* sector), and prepared to initiate operations.

The Pfalz did not enjoy a good start in the *Jasta,* as Dannhüber himself crashed at Thugny during a practice flight in a D IIIa on 11 February and went to the hospital. Fortunately for the future of the *Staffel,* his replacement was Ltn d R Hans Böhning. An accomplished Bavarian, Böhning was born on 6 July 1893 in Grottau-Reichenberg and had served in a Bavarian field artillery regiment prior to joining the *Fliegertruppe.*

From 26 April to 3 July 1917 he flew with Bavarian Fl. Abt. (A) 290. After *Jagdflieger* training Böhning was posted to *Jasta* 36 on 3 July 1917, where he attained his first four successes. On 6 November 1917 he was assigned to *Jasta* 76b and shot down a Sopwith on 1 December for his fifth claim. Böhning then followed Dannhüber to *Staffel* 79b and took over the unit on 23 February. The unit moved north to the 18. *Armee,* near St Quentin, as Operation *Michael* loomed. It settled in at Villers le Sec as part of *Jagdgruppe* 12 (*Staffeln* 24, 44 and 79b), commanded by Heinrich Kroll.

On the second day of the Offensive (22 March), Böhning led his Pfalz *Staffel* into combat against the RAF and opened his unit's score book in a spectacular manner. Both the *Staffelführer* and Ltn d R Wilhelm Buchstett received confirmation for one SE 5 each, downed at Vermand. Although there are some discrepancies in the details, it seems likely that Böhning's opponent was Capt R W Howard MC of No 2 Sqn Australian Flying Corps (AFC), who was a flight commander with eight victories. Howard and his patrol had dived on a two-seater when they were in turn jumped by a number of German fighters, and the Australian ace was brought down mortally wounded near Epehy.

The *Staffel* was back in action against the RFC on the 24th, but came up short. Buchstett claimed a 'Sopwith' once again near Vermand but failed to receive confirmation, while Gefr Linus Luger was wounded and left for the hospital. In the next two days the *Jagdgruppe* advanced to the former British airfield at Villeselve. Böhning closed out March by downing a French two-seater at Varennes on the 31st.

April began successfully as Buchstett chalked up a SPAD for his second *Luftsieg,* but Uffz Müller was wounded and taken prisoner the same day. On 6 April, Böhning brought his tally to nine with an RE 8 confirmed south of Noyon at 1000 hrs. Buchstett's burgeoning career was abruptly

In the late spring and summer of 1918 *Jasta* 79b was a component of *Jagdgruppe* 12, which was commanded by the *Pour le Mérite* ace Ltn d R Heinrich Kroll – another element of the *Gruppe* was Saxon *Jasta* 24, also led by Kroll. The 30-victory ace Kroll had plenty of experience with the Pfalz D III and D IIIa himself. The *Jasta* 24 war diary survives (thanks to Alex Imrie), and it records a litany of complaints and accidents involving Pfalz aircraft. Kroll himself took over the first Pfalz (D III 4009/17) to arrive at *Jasta* 24 on 27 September 1917. On 25 October the *Jasta* war diary recorded that, 'The type is slower than the Albatros D III. It is fast in a dive and is then faster than the Albatros D V. The climb performance varies greatly, sometimes almost as good as an average Albatros D V but never better. It is not advisable for the unit to be equipped with both the Pfalz D III and the Albatros D V. However, the Pfalz by itself in one *Staffel* could be successful'. On 25 January Kroll achieved a victory in D IIIa 4286/17 when he shot down a Bristol for his 17th victim, but he then suffered the loss of half of his left aileron in a dive, as mentioned earlier. Upon landing safely, he immediately telephoned *Kofl* 18, Hptm Blumberg, to complain about the quality of the Pfalz machines. He was promised delivery of three Fokker Dr Is, but these never showed up, and his unit soldiered on with Pfalz and Albatros until they picked up D VIIs on 28 May

halted on the 11th when he, too, was taken PoW, the victim of SPA 75 ace Sous Lt William Herisson who shot down his Pfalz D IIIa near Marqueglise. The next day Böhning balanced the scales somewhat with a SPAD for his ninth score.

Future Pfalz ace Ltn Roman Schneider, who was born in Passau, Bavaria, on 9 August 1898, had served in the 16th Bavarian Infantry Regiment prior to making the switch to aviation. His *Jagdflieger* career nearly ended before it began due to an alarming accident that occurred during this period. He wrote (translated by O'Brien Browne);

'It was towards the end of April 1918 as *Staffel* 79, under the leadership of Ltn Böhning, ran up against two opponents flying at about 100 metres under our *Kette* over Montdidier at 3700 metres. Ltn Böhning attacked downwards in a steep bank, and in this way broke up our *Kette* which was following him. Thus it came about that my neighbours on the left of the *Kette* – I was flying on the right – suddenly flew towards me. I could just avoid the first one by rapidly diving my Pfalz D IIIa machine, but with the second one, this did not work. There was a huge crash, and the end of my right wing appeared as if it had been shaved off from the strut joint outwards. Simultaneously, my aircraft and I began to spin ever more rapidly along the aeroplane's longitudinal axis. Ltn (Fritz Edler) von Braun – my fellow sufferer – was lying exactly in a very sharp bank and had taken half of my right wing off with his wing.

'During these spins, my aeroplane slowly went over on its nose and was soon rushing on at high speed. Now, I really did not want to give up with a fatal crash as my fate – I could quite easily have jumped out – without at least having tried to get my aeroplane under control again. The first thing I had to do was to free my machine from this crazy spinning. And that was the catch. Through the violent departure of my right aileron, the control cable joints were also wrecked and the joystick could not be moved either to the left or to the right. First, a rather powerful jerk by me freed the control cables. Soon I was also able, by means of the still-functioning left aileron, to bring my machine into a somewhat stable position.

'Gradually I pulled my machine back into a horizontal position – which caused me no little worry – and slowly but surely I flew my aeroplane to my airfield, where, immediately upon landing, I was surrounded by a crowd of incredulous people who would believe that this aircraft had been flown in this condition only after the repeated affirmations of witnesses. Ltn von Braun then brought me some pieces of my aeroplane that had been pulled out of one of his wings after he landed.'

Misfortune continued on 2 May as a *Jasta* 79b patrol came out on the wrong end of an encounter with several French SPAD aces. Vfw Phillip Jopp's Pfalz was sent flaming to earth near Montdidier at 2000 hrs, apparently the victim of Sous Lt Andre Barcat and others of SPA 153, as well as Capitaine Auguste Lahoulle of SPA 154. Ltn Edler von Braun was once again lucky, escaping with a light wound after he was attacked by Lt Henri Hay de Slade of SPA 86. Fortunately, that evening 23-year-old Vfw Ludwig Walk arrived as a replacement – but the *Staffel* was still badly understrength at only six pilots.

Throughout May Böhning struggled to lead his inexperienced *Staffel* through the deadly learning curve which all fighter pilots must endure, as they repeatedly encountered large formations of superior French aircraft.

His initials forming his personal marking, Ltn d R Hans Böhning poses with Pfalz D IIIa 8170/17. This machine was his mount as *Staffelführer* of *Jasta* 79b in the spring of 1918. The wings were covered in five-colour printed camouflage fabric and the fuselage was painted in an unrecorded dark colour. This certainly seems darker than the usual shade of 'Bavarian blue', and is thus assumed to have been black. Note the rack for flare cartridges just over Böhning's shoulder and a tubular sight mounted between the machine guns – a portion of the fuselage *Balkenkreuz* emblem is also just visible. Böhning may have scored as many as seven victories flying a D IIIa in *Jasta* 79b, making him – along with Rudolf Stark – a true Pfalz ace

Things began to look up on the 13th as the *Jasta* celebrated the award of the 'Hohenzollern' to their *Staffelführer*. On the next day Schneider gained the first of his five victories when he downed an AR 2 at Courcelles. Böhning reached the ranks of the ten-victory *Kanonen* on the 15th by bringing the SPAD XIII of Sous Lt Matrat of SPA 154 down intact behind German lines – the SPAD was brought to the *Staffel* field at Ercheu as a trophy, but Matrat soon died of his wounds. Eight days later Schneider gained his second *Luftsieg* (a 'Bristol' at Tricot).

The *Jasta* lost four pilots in June in exchange for only two victories, as the inferiority of their Pfalz became ever more obvious. At about 1912 hrs on the 20th, Böhning and some of his men attacked an antiquated French Sopwith 1A2 (a design even older than the Pfalz) from the artillery-spotting *Escadrille* SOP 270. The crew of Aspirant Bos and Cpl Digeon still managed to down the Pfalz of Vfw Bergmann, who was killed. Böhning then bored in to riddle the Sopwith, and pilot Bos was killed and Digeon wounded as they crashed at Autheuil for the Bavarian's 12th tally.

As July began Böhning left on leave and Schneider took acting command of the *Jasta*. He proved himself worthy on the 2nd when he destroyed a SPAD XIII (probably from SPA 159) and chalked up his third score with a Sopwith on the 18th. The inexperience of his pilots and the inadequacies of their Pfalz still took a toll, however. Flg Stefan Meier was killed during a test flight on the 5th, and Gefr Luger – having recovered from his wounding in March – crashed fatally just after take-off from Ercheu on the 19th.

Ltn Böhning returned on the last day of July, and the situation improved as the unit started to receive D VIIs. Böhning would take his score to 17 before a hip wound sidelined him on 20 September. Schneider, too, survived the war with five victories to his credit. Post-war, Böhning remained active in aviation as an engineer and glider pilot until he was killed in a glider crash on 22 October 1934.

THE WORKHORSE

oon after the USA entered World War I in April 1917, propagandists were making wild claims about the massive numbers of aircraft that American industry would soon be adding to the war effort. In Germany, *Kogenluft (Kommandierenden General der Luftstreitkräfte)* realized these claims were greatly exaggerated, but still considered the threat posed by American intervention as a serious one.

To counter this, on 23 June 1917 *Kogenluft* introduced an expansion plan that became known as the *Amerikaprogramm.* It called for a 100 percent increase in the number of *Jagdstaffeln* from 40 to 80. This placed a tremendous strain on both the German aircraft industry and the pool of experienced fighter pilots. Many of the *Amerikaprogramm Jastas* would be forced to carry out their duties far below their intended strength in both aircraft and airmen.

Although the Pfalz D III/IIIa design had its faults, the demand for fighter aircraft was great. The impressive production capabilities of the Pfalz factory (producing 793 aeroplanes in 1917 and 1850 in 1918) meant that the D IIIa would see widespread service. The aircraft was available in quantity, and provided fairly reliable, if not superior, service. Thus it soldiered on well into the summer of 1918 – far longer than it should have. Even so, in the hands of a skilled and experienced *Jagdflieger* the Pfalz could still deliver substantial results. This will be evident in the following text, which will start by covering the 4. *Armee Staffeln* in Flanders and then work its way southeast along the Western Front.

Jasta 7

For much of its existence *Jasta* 7 flew with the 4. *Armee* in Flanders and was commanded by Ltn d R Josef Jacobs, the celebrated Fokker Dr I ace. While Jacobs is best known for his black Fokker triplanes, he occasionally flew Pfalz aircraft, as did others in his *Staffel.* Researcher Stephen Lawson has shown that the first mention of a Pfalz D III in Jacobs' diary occurs on 28 September 1917, when the unit was based at Aertrycke. 'Yesterday, the first Pfalz arrived. It appears to climb better and be more manoeuvrable'. Jacobs was presumably comparing the Pfalz to the Albatros D V.

The next day he wrote, 'This afternoon my first Pfalz arrived'. On 4 October, 'Today I flew my Pfalz D III for the first time. It climbs better but is slower'. On the 15th, the *Staffel* received two Pfalz and two D Vs from AFP 4 in Ghent, and the unit continued to operate a mix of both types. The D IIIa was still in use with *Jasta* 7 nine months later.

One ace besides Jacobs who flew the Pfalz in *Jasta* 7 was Ltn Carl Degelow. Born in Munsterdorf on 5 January 1891, Degelow had seen extensive infantry service before flying two-seaters with F. Fl. Abt. (A) 216 in 1917. After training on fighters, he was posted to *Jasta* 36 on 17 August, but within four days Degelow was sent off in disgrace after accidentally wounding a groundcrewman during practice gunnery. He luckily obtained a second chance with *Jasta* 7, and had been determined to prove himself under

A clutch of warmly bundled *Jasta* 7 pilots poses for a photograph beneath the wing of a Pfalz fighter circa late December 1917. Standing, from left to right, are Vfw Swoboda, Ltn d R Paul Billik (31 victories), Vfw Rudolf Lander, Ltn d R Paul Lotz (4), Ltn d R Max Hillmann (1), Ltn d R Mühlen, Obflgmtr Kurt Schönfelder (13), Ltn d R Carl Degelow (30) and Vfw Hans Horst (4). Seated in front are Ltn d R Hermann Kunz (6), *Staffelführer* Ltn d R Josef Jacobs (41 to 47 victories) and Ltn Otto Kunst (1). Of these, at least Jacobs, Lotz and Degelow are thought to have flown a Pfalz occasionally in *Jasta* 7, while Billik flew the D IIIa with great success later in *Jasta* 52

Ltn d R Degelow's *Jasta* 7 Pfalz D IIIa was written off in this accident. According to historian S T Lawson, this is probably the incident recorded in Jacobs' diary on 23 March 1918, as Degelow raced against a strong wind when landing and turned his aircraft over but remained unscathed. The fuselage, struts, wheels and (apparently) all upper wing surfaces were painted in *Jasta* 7 black. Degelow's famous personal emblem of the 'white stag' was painted in silvery-white, with golden yellow antlers and hooves

the skilled tutelage of Jacobs. Only two days after his arrival on 1 September, Degelow forced a Camel down but failed to achieve a confirmed victory. On 8 December *Jasta* 7 tangled with 'Sopwiths' over Passchendaele. Jacobs and Degelow were both credited with 'forced to land' victims, but these were not credited as official victories by German standards.

Jacobs and his *Staffel* clashed with No 10 Naval Squadron on 12 December. Ace Paul Billik shot a Camel down behind German lines, but Degelow's similar claim was disallowed. On 25 January Degelow wounded the crew of a Bristol from No 20 Sqn, who landed their F 2B near Kortemarck to be taken PoW. By March he was flying a Pfalz D IIIa, and according to the research of Stephen Lawson, apparently wrecked it on the 23rd. Jacobs' diary reported, 'Upon landing, Ltn Degelow raced against a 30 kph wind. Machine turned over and he remained completely unhurt'. In June Degelow was transferred to *Jasta* 40.

Another *Jasta* 7 ace that may have flown a Pfalz at times was Ltn d R Paul Lotz, a 22-year-old from Rumenau. He claimed a Camel from No 70 Sqn at Ramscapelle on 18 October 1917 for his first victory. Exactly two months later he doubled his score with another Camel, then destroyed a DH 4 from No 57 Sqn near Courtrai on 24 January. On 12 April 1918 he shot down an Armstrong-Whitworth FK 8 from No 10 Sqn north of Bailleul for his fourth triumph.

Eleven days later Lotz was part of an evening patrol led by Jacobs in his triplane that flew about five miles into enemy territory. Jacobs wrote that Lotz and Uffz Böhne were attacked by four SEs. These were a group from No 74 Sqn led by 'Mick' Mannock, who attacked the Pfalz at the rear of the formation and pumped three short bursts into it at close range. J I T 'Taffy' Jones of No 74 Sqn stated that this Pfalz 'was highly coloured with a black body, white-tipped tail, silver and black chequered top planes', and that it turned over on its back and went down smoking badly.

Actually, Jacobs reported that 'Uffz Böhne turned on his back, Ltn Lotz came to his assistance and was caught obliquely from below and received a wound in the leg. He was able to fly all the way home and was brought to Marcke hospital. Uffz Böhne's machine was severely shot up'. Lotz was not badly injured, for he soon took over *Jasta* 44. There, he brought his score to ten, before being killed in a flying accident on 23 October.

Uffz Max Mertens was one of *Jasta* 7's 'near aces' who had a brief but eventful career flying a black Pfalz D IIIa, possibly with green personal markings. Having joined the *Staffel* on 16 April 1918, Mertens settled in quickly and received credit for a balloon north of Ypres on 14 May. On 17 June he claimed a Dolphin south of Dickebusch Lake, but this was denied in favour of another pilot. Mertens had better luck the next day when he attained his second confirmed *Luftsieg* over a Camel in the same area at 0920 hrs. Then came the evening of the 19th – Jacobs wrote;

'Uffz Eigenbrodt and Uffz Mertens took off for a balloon attack. At 4000 metres altitude the two crossed the lines, and in spite of a colossal flak barrage, Uffz Mertens attacked a balloon and probably brought it down.'

Mertens had unluckily made his attack at a time when No 74 Sqn's SEs and No 4 Sqn AFC's Camels were in the area. 'Taffy' Jones wrote of, 'the German balloon-strafer, whose reckless courage we all admired. He had shot down one of our balloons near Hazebrouck, and so elated was he with his success that he decided to attack another. In a few moments he was trapped, although a comrade who had been more observant had cleared off. In one sense it was a sad sight to watch the trapped enemy's vain but heroic efforts to get away'.

Finally the Australian ace Capt A H Cobby took lethal aim at Mertens' Pfalz, and he later recalled, 'I got on his tail and put about a hundred rounds into him from point-blank range, and he crashed into the forest of Nieppe, on our side of the lines.'

Jones wrote, 'There followed a sort of target practice. Machine after machine dived and gave a burst at it before zooming steeply upwards'.

Afterwards, Mertens' battered body was brought back to No 74 Sqn's airfield, and the RAF pilots all commented on his unusual clothing. He was wearing a swallow-tailed coat and grey flannel trousers – perhaps he had left a *Jasta* party just before his balloon mission. The shattered wreckage of the D IIIa was given the number G/2Bde/16, and it was reported that the fuselage and uppersurfaces of the wings were painted black and dark green, with undersides in silver.

Jasta 20

Jagdstaffel 20, commanded by Ltn Joachim von Busse (who survived the war with a tally of 11) also flew the Pfalz in Flanders. The *Jasta* was

Ltn Raven Freiherr von Barnekow appears every inch the dashing young nobleman in this early portrait, in which he wears an uhlan 'Tschapka' helmet. Von Barnekow downed his first five opponents in *Jasta* 20 and may have flown a Pfalz D IIIa for at least the first two or three of these – he survived the war with 11 victories. His Pfalz D IIIa was probably painted in *Jasta* 20 brown on the fuselage with a white rudder narrowly outlined in red, with his initial 'B' on the fuselage. Von Barnekow's close friendship with Ernst Udet continued after the war. The two met again in June 1933 when Udet came to New York, and von Barnekow had just started working for General Motors there. Shortly after World War 2 began, von Barnekow managed to reach Germany from New York, sailing in a cargo ship. Hans-Georg von der Osten recalled that von Barnekow served with him on the staff of General Kurt von Döring, whom both had known in their old *Jasta* 4 days. 'He (von Barnekow) was on very friendly terms with Udet and he had knowledge of Udet's suicide. This made a deep impression on him, and a short time later, on his parents' estate, he took his own life by putting a bullet in his head' (*HAC/UTD*)

completely equipped with the D III and D IIIa, possibly from March to June 1918. On 17 March Vfw Otto Schulz was killed in a D III crash at Douai during a practice flight.

Raven Freiherr von Barnekow, whom we first met in *Jasta* 4, had transferred to *Jasta* 20 in late February. Although he had claimed no victories to that point, he would achieve his first success in his new unit when he downed an SE 5 on 12 May. Von Barnekow's victim was seven-victory ace Lt Henry Dolan of No 74 Sqn, who was shot down out of 'Mick' Mannock's flight over Wulverghem.

Von Barnekow's comrade Ltn d R Johannes Gildemeister scored his first *Luftsieg* of an eventual five on 21 May – a Camel (possibly from No 73 Sqn) south of Bailleul. Eight days later von Barnekow added another SE 5 north of Bailleul for his second score. On the 31st *Jasta* 20 again tangled with SEs over Laventie at 1640 hrs, with Ltn d R Helten claiming one while Ltn Bucholz was wounded in the same combat.

On 6 June the *Staffel* was relocated to Menin in the 4. *Armee*, where it became part of *Jagdgruppe* 6 along with *Jagdstaffeln* 7, 16b, 40, 51 and 56. Pilots of JgGrp 6 continually found themselves in combat with the Camels of No 4 Sqn AFC and the SEs of Mannock's No 74 Sqn – the leading British ace seemed to harbour a grudge against the Pfalz, claiming at least 18 of the type. On the 9 June Gefr Heinz Kleineberg's Pfalz D IIIa 1306/18 was apparently shot down, but he avoided Allied captivity by landing his aircraft intact at Schoondijke, Zeeland, in the Netherlands, where both he and his machine were interned.

On 12 June the *Jasta* attacked a patrol of Camels from No 4 Sqn AFC at 1300 hrs, with mixed results. The official Australian history reports;

'The patrol was promptly attacked in turn by nine Albatros and Pfalz scouts. (Capt E J K) McCloughry turned upon one Pfalz that was diving at him, fired a burst into the enemy's side at 30 yards' range, and the Pfalz went down out of control. It was seen by AA observers to crash. Martin was not so fortunate – a Pfalz shot him down from above, and he fell in No-Man's Land near Meteren and was killed.'

Lt W S Martin fell to von Barnekow, who achieved his third victory, while his comrade Ltn d R Helten was apparently McCloughry's victim – the first of 21 for the Australian.

Three days later von Barnekow almost became a victim himself – of 'friendly fire' from a German ace! Josef Jacobs and his *Jasta* 7 pilots were on a morning sortie from 0845 to 1050 hrs when, according to Jacobs;

'I picked on one of three SE 5s flying at a higher level patrol, but immediately a second SE 5 hurtled down at me. As he passed by, a second aircraft, whom I thought to be a Frenchman because of a white and red rudder, zipped by as well. I cartwheeled over and opened up with my guns, and, as I levelled off, I immediately saw that I was firing point blank into a Pfalz D IIIa which I recognised to be a *Jagdstaffel* 20

On 11 June Gefr Heinz Kleineberg of *Jasta* 20 landed at Schoondijke, in the Netherlands, and his D IIIa 1306/18 was interned (there is a small discrepancy in the Dutch records, which give the date as 12 June). This *Jasta* 20 Pfalz was probably painted in dark brown on the fuselage and upper tail surfaces. This, along with a white rudder, was the unit marking of *Jasta* 20 recorded in August. The wings would probably have been covered in five-colour printed fabric

machine because on the side of the fuselage there appeared a large letter "B" for Ltn von Barnekow. Later in the day I phoned and apologised for my impulsive action, and was grateful to learn that his aircraft had not been seriously damaged by my machine gun fire.'

Indeed, von Barnekow's Pfalz could not have been too badly damaged, for he claimed one of the SEs east of Ypres for his fourth victory.

By early July *Jasta* 20 was re-equipping with Fokker D VIIs. On the 13th Ltn d R Karl Plauth crashed in a Fokker. Having survived this incident with light injuries, he wrote;

'My concern now only with a new Fokker, as I have, despite great enthusiasm, no desire to fly an Albatros or a Pfalz at the Front.'

Jasta 40s

In mid-May 1918 Carl Degelow was transferred from *Jasta* 7 to Royal Saxon *Jasta* 40, also in the 4. *Armee*. He wrote;

'I was assigned to *Jasta* 40, which was then at a small field near Lille, not far from *Jasta* 7's airfield. Indeed, we often flew together during joint operations. When I arrived at *Jasta* 40 in May 1918, the *Staffel* was equipped with Albatros D Va and Pfalz D IIIa aircraft. Given the choice, I selected the Pfalz D IIIa – a type I had also flown in *Jasta* 7. The Pfalz was a bit underpowered, and it did not climb as well as the Albatros, but I felt it was a safer aircraft.

'For some time the Albatros D Va had a structural problem with the lower wing spar, which had a tendency to break under stress, causing the bottom wing to part company with the rest of the aeroplane. Pilots were still instructed to avoid getting into a very stressful dive, which is one of the best ways to save your own hide when you are on the losing end of an aerial combat. Suffice to say, this did little to instill confidence in the Albatros fighter aeroplanes. So, in my case, I took the second-rate Pfalz and, having learned its limitations, made the best of a bad job.'

In late April 1918 Uffz Werner Hertel was posted to Saxon *Jasta* 40, where he was later photographed with his mechanics and this D IIIa. The Pfalz displays the unit colours of a black fuselage, struts and wheel covers, as well as a white tail unit. The machine does not yet bear any personal insignia on the fuselage, but a flare cartridge rack has been affixed near the cockpit and an anemometer is attached to the port interplane strut. The wings were covered in five-colour printed camouflage fabric (*Courtesy C Minx*)

With the commander Ltn d R Dilthey on leave, Degelow led the *Staffel* in his 'second-rate' Pfalz for the latter half of May. One of his wingmen was Uffz Werner Hertel, who had been posted to the unit in late April. Hertel also flew a D IIIa, his machine boasting a beautiful winged dagger emblem on the black fuselage.

On 18 June Degelow achieved his lone Pfalz victory in *Jasta* 40 and 'made ace' with an SE 5 destroyed at 0930 hrs over Vieux Berquin. His next victory, on 25 June, would be his first of 25 claimed in a D VII. The *Staffel* retained a few Pfalz and Albatros for awhile, but the unit's aces no doubt received Fokkers as soon as possible.

Marine Feld Jagdstaffeln

Along with the army *Staffeln* described already, the land-based naval airmen of the first three *Marine Feld Jagdstaffeln* (MFJ) also flew Pfalz fighters on the 4. *Armee* front. The records of MFJ I, II and III provide ample evidence that both the D III and D IIIa were supplied to these units. However, it is difficult to ascertain if any of the more noted naval aces ever achieved many victories on the type.

MFJ I, commanded by Gotthard Sachsenberg, received its first Pfalz on 5 October 1917 when D III 4023/17 arrived. Eight days later, five more

D IIIs were taken on (as well as two Albatros D Vs) in exchange for four older Albatros. The unit was never fully equipped with either the Pfalz D III or D IIIa, and neither was MFJ II, which would be commanded by 'Theo' Osterkamp after March 1918. MFJ III was formed in June 1918, and is thought to have gone into combat largely equipped with the D IIIa, although some Albatros were probably also on hand.

MFJ II pilot Flgmt Arnim Undi-ener was killed at Saeskerke in Pfalz D III 4169/17 on 28 January 1918.

A spectacular group of highly personalised D IIIa machines from a naval *Jasta* is seen in this rare line-up photo taken at Jabbeke-Snellegem – again, the unit is likely MFJ III. The dark-painted noses displayed on some of these Pfalz were probably yellow, while the tail of the machine in the foreground *may* have been yellow and white. A variety of individual markings is in evidence (*courtesy E Lambrecht*)

Ltn d R Walter Kypke was commander of *Jasta* 47w throughout its existence. Another bespectacled, yet deadly, German airman, Kypke came to his command with six victories, and would add three more (at least two in a Pfalz) with his new *Staffel*. Here, he proudly displays his Knight's Cross of the Hohenzollern House Order on his tunic, along with his Iron Cross and Pilot's Badge

On 26 March, a group of four Camels from No 4 Naval Squadron dived from 17,000 ft onto what they described as a formation of Pfalz fighters. Flight Commander R M Keirstead (13 victories) and Flt Sub Lt Hickey both fired at various Pfalz in the dogfight, and were soon joined by three Belgian Hanriots from the 9me *Escadrille*, flown by Lt A de Meulemeester, Adjt Baron G Kervyn de Lettenhove and Sous Lt Baron G deMevius. Obflgmt Hans Groth's Pfalz D IIIa 5923/17 was shot down and Groth was killed – credit for his fate was shared by all three Belgians.

MFJ II commander 'Theo' Osterkamp and Flgmt Eduard Blaas were apparently in this fight, for Osterkamp claimed a Camel for his eighth success and Blaas downed another for the first of his five victories. The No 4 Naval Squadron pilots involved claimed three Pfalz 'crashed' or 'destroyed', but all these claims refer to Groth, who was the only casualty.

Almost exactly one month later, on 25 April, another MFJ II Pfalz fell to the Hanriot pilots of the 9me *Escadrille*. Flgobmt Bruno Feitzmann was killed in Pfalz D IIIa 5942/17, shot down by Kervyn de Lettenhove and G de Mevius at Boitshoucke. Unfortunately, little else concerning the naval Pfalz pilots can be ascertained.

Jasta 47w

The tale of Royal Württemberg *Jasta* 47 is typical of many struggling units of the *Amerikaprogramm*. The *Staffel* was formed in late December 1917, and on the 26th left FEA 10 at Böblingen for its first station in Flanders, at Harlebeke, in the 4. *Armee*. The unit was fortunate to receive a full complement of 20 Pfalz D IIIa fighters, serials 5902 through 5921/17. The *Staffel* was also lucky in the choice of its first, and only, commander, Ltn d R Walter Kypke – an accomplished *Jagdflieger*.

Born on 22 September 1892 in Stettin, Kypke had volunteered for No 3 *Magdeburg Infanterie Regt* 66 at the outset of the war. He obtained leave to take pilot's training as early as October 1914. After a considerable training regimen Kypke went to the front in *Fokkerstaffel Falkenhausen* in *Armee Abteilung* 'A'. By the time that unit was modified into the new *Jasta* 14 in September 1916, he already had his first victory, and would gain valuable experience under the stern guidance of Oblt Rudolf Berthold. Posted to *Jasta* 41 in August 1917, Kypke had soon added four more to his tally whilst serving with the unit.

His first command was *Kest* 5, being appointed its leader in early November 1917. Kypke gained an additional victory there before taking command of *Jasta* 47w. He was allowed to bring along four experienced pilots from *Kest* 5 to form the nucleus of his new *Staffel,* one of these being Vfw Friedrich Ehmann, who would gain eight victories under Kypke's tutelage. Two of the other ex-*Kest* 5 airmen were soon transferred back to their previous unit, and the rest of the *Staffel* airmen were green 'kids' fresh from the *Jastaschulen.*

Before the *Staffel* could really get its feet wet, it lost one of the two remaining experienced pilots. Vfw Schille crashed badly from 50 metres as he was testing Pfalz D IIIa 5904/17, 'as a result of misfiring of the engine,' according to the war diary (translated by S T Lawson). On 9 March the unit relocated to Bevren, where it joined *Jastas* 7, 28w and 51 in *Jagdgruppe* 6.

First blood for the new *Staffel* went to Ehmann on the 11th when he downed a 'Sopwith' southwest of Zonnebeke – it was last seen diving away smoking badly. On 17 March the *Jasta* tally rose to three when Ehmann claimed a 'DH 5' (sic) near Moorslede and Gefr Gebhardt was credited with a Sopwith near Staden. The very next day Ehmann scored again. A massed formation of twelve Nieuport 27s of No 29 Sqn were met by ten German fighters from *Jastas* 47 and 51 southwest of Roulers. Josef Jacobs was a witness;

'We went out again at 1150 hrs, at which time two Pfalz of *Jasta* 47 caught a Camel (sic) above our field. The Englishman spun in, straightened out and again spun downwards and, at about 1200 metres altitude, rolled over and went down low behind the houses at Rumbeke, clear to the ground. There he zoomed up and disappeared behind the trees. The Pfalz finally nailed him, and he crashed in a meadow.'

Ehmann's opponent was Lt L A Edens, who died when his Nieuport 27 B6836 'exploded' near Hooglede. *Jasta* 51 also accounted for another No 29 Sqn aircraft. The RFC pilots claimed at least five Pfalz scouts downed, but no German airmen or aircraft were lost in the engagement.

On 29 March the *Jasta* was moved south to take up residence at Fachez in the 6. *Armee.* It would serve first in JgGrp 7 and next in JgGrp 3 as the fighter *Staffeln* were shifted about to provide assistance for the Lys Offensive. Here, *Jasta* 47w sustained its most successful stretch of the war. No less than three victories were achieved on 12 April. First Ehmann riddled a Camel near Frelingham at 1020 hrs for his fourth tally and Ltn Haevernik felled another Sopwith 30 minutes later. One of these was flown by Lt A C Dean, whose No 43 Sqn Camel suffered a hit to the engine, forcing him down – he sustained a broken nose and was taken PoW. The *Jasta* war diary reported;

'In the course of the violent air battle Ehmann got some hits in the

Although this blemished photograph has been captioned as showing pilots of *Jasta* 47w, the author believes it to actually depict airmen of *Kest* 5. Several of these pilots would soon transfer to the newly formed *Jasta* 47w. According to the original caption, tentatively identified as seated in the front row, from left to right, are Ltn d R Franz Piechulek, Ltn d R Walter Kypke and Vzfw Heidfeld. In the back row are a dimly seen Gefr Schille, Vzfw Fritz von Puttkamer, possibly Uffz Faukl, Offz Stv Bansmer and an almost invisible Vzfw Friedrich Ehmann at extreme right. Kypke would shortly take command of *Staffel* 47w, and he would bring along Bansmer, Heidfeld, Ehmann and Schille to form the experienced nucleus of his new *Jasta*. Bansmer and Heidfeld soon returned to *Kest* 5, however, and Schille was severely injured in a crash on 9 February. Ehmann would stay on to become the star of the *Jasta* with eight confirmed claims *(HAC/UTD)*

radiator and had to make an emergency landing near Frehlingen, in the frontlines, during which the aircraft rolled over and was heavily damaged.'

Finally, on the 12th Kypke was credited with an RE 8 south of Estaires. This was likely C4555 of No 4 Sqn, and its observer, 2Lt D Henderson was wounded in the leg but made it home safely. Five days later Haevernik brought down another RE 8, and on the 20th Gebhardt gained his second *Luftsieg* with an SE 5 west of Vieux Berquin.

21 April – the day Richthofen fell – was also a momentous date for Friedrich Ehmann. He was credited with his fifth victory at 1625 hrs German time. Many historians feel that Ehmann's opponent was Camel B6319, which was flown by none other than No 203 Sqn's renowned Capt Robert A Little.

The ranking Australian ace reported that he shot a Pfalz scout down 'out of control' near Vieux Berquin at 1500 hrs British time (one hour behind German time), then was jumped by another fighter and had his main spar holed and controls shot up – he made a forced landing south of Hazebrouck, behind Allied lines. The Pfalz pilot he shot down for his 44th victory was likely Vfw Erich Kauffmann of *Jasta* 47w, who was badly wounded and died the following day.

The unit's string of successes had ended, and misfortune ensued. On 25 April Pfalz D IIIa 8015/17 was destroyed when Ltn Käser made a forced landing. Ltn d R Determeyer suffered severe back injuries on 2 May when his D IIIa 8338/17 was shot down by SE 5 pilot Capt H A Rigby of No 1 Sqn. Two days later the *Staffel* moved to Lomme airfield, near Lille. On 11 May, the Pfalz nemesis 'Mick' Mannock of No 74 Sqn pounced on D IIIa 5916/17 over Deulemont on the Lys and shot it out of the sky in flames at 1835 hrs. The unfortunate pilot was newly arrived Ltn d R Otto Aeckerle, a neophyte who died one day before his 24th birthday. Mannock described his victim as a 'Pfalz single seater. Coloured silver and black, with red nose'.

Further tragedy befell the *Jasta* on 18 May when an intense bombing raid by No 206 Sqn struck Lomme. Pfalz D IIIa 1259/18 was destroyed, three others damaged and three mechanics were wounded. Four days later the *Staffel* lost Ltn Breuer when he was wounded, probably by the irrepressible 'Taffy' Jones of No 74 Sqn. On 25 May Kypke initiated a reversal of fortunes when he downed an RE 8 at Beythen for his eighth success, and claimed an unconfirmed Dolphin three days later. Also on the 28th, Ehmann successfully sent an SE 5 down smoking badly at Vlamertinghe for his sixth triumph.

By 6 June the *Jasta* was at Lieramont in the 2. *Armee*. Two days later, yet another new pilot was killed when Ltn d R Erlewein's Pfalz D IIIa was shot down by British fighters. On 9 July *Jasta* 47w was transferred south to the 3. *Armee* and was then part of *Jagdgruppe* 9. Ltn Kypke's ninth, and final victory (a SPAD VII), came on 16 July.

It is not known exactly when the unit attained its first D VIIs, but some were on hand by August/September. Ehmann also survived the war, credited with eight victories – perhaps seven scored on a Pfalz. He was the last *Jagdflieger* of the war to be awarded the Gold Military Merit Medal, receiving it on 18 October 1918. That same day Kypke received the Württemberg Friedrich Order, he too being the last fighter pilot to do so.

The *Staffelführer* of *Jagdstaffel* 52 from its inception until 10 August 1918 was Ltn d R Paul Billik, one of the least known of all the high-scoring German aces. Having learned his trade under the skilful teaching of Adolf von Tutschek in *Jasta* 12 and Josef Jacobs in *Jasta* 7, Billik led *Staffel* 52 with great success. He and his pilots made optimum use of their Pfalz D IIIa machines against some of the best RAF fighter squadrons. Billik scored the last 22 of his 31 victories in *Jasta* 52 before he was taken PoW on 10 August. Rather unjustly, his captivity denied him a well-earned 'Blue Max'

Jasta 52

One *Amerikaprogramm* unit that did quite well with the Pfalz D IIIa was *Jasta* 52, proudly known as the *'Schwarzen Staffel'* (the black squadron). This unit was formed at FEA 7 in Braunschweig, and it went into combat equipped entirely with the Pfalz D IIIa. Its commander was the formidable Ltn d R Paul Billik, who then had eight victories.

Billik was born in Haatsch, in Silesia, on 27 March 1891. Having served in *Infanterie-Regiment* 157, he transferred to the *Fliegertruppe* in May 1916. Billik was posted to *Schutzstaffel* 4 in January 1917, and flew two-seaters with that unit through March. His first fighter pilot experience came in *Jasta* 12, where he learnt his trade under the masterful example of Adolf von Tutschek, scoring four victories in three months. On 4 July Billik was posted to *Jasta* 7, and became one of Josef Jacobs' most valued pilots. He would follow Jacobs' example of aggressive leadership in the air – and the black colour scheme for his unit's aircraft – when he took over *Jasta* 52.

On 7 February 1918 the 'Black *Staffel*' moved to Bersée airfield in the 6. *Armee.* The first event of note occurred on 6 March 1918, when Gefr Walther Conderet was killed in Pfalz D IIIa 4236/17 northwest of Lens at 1525 hrs. He fell to the guns of No 40 Sqn's Capt R J Tipton, and his D IIIa was given the British number 'G 146'. Three days later *Jasta* 52 again tangled with No 40 Sqn, Billik downing one SE at Malmaison at 1704 hrs and another six minutes later over Noyelles. No 40 Sqn lost its CO, Maj L A Tilney, killed (probably by Billik), had Lt O La T Foster taken PoW and Capt Tipton wounded. In exchange, however, *Jasta* 52's Ltn d R Nissen also died.

On 28 March Billik again achieved a double. One of his opponents was probably Lt C M Feez of No 2 Sqn AFC, who was taken PoW when his Sopwith came down southeast of Arras. On 7 April Billik triumphed over yet another Camel for his 13th victory.

Another *Jasta* 52 ace was Vfw Hermann Juhnke, born on 7 April 1893 in Laurenberg. Before the war he had served in *Luftschiffer-Battailon* Nr 1, then transferred to heavier-than-air aviation in July 1915. Following his flight training he joined Fl. Abt. (A) 238 and flew with this unit for a year (and earned the Golden Military Merit Cross), then went to *Jastaschule* I on 30 August 1917. Juhnke's first fighter unit was *Jasta* 41, after which he flew with *Kest* 5, before being posted to *Jasta* 52 on 4 March 1918. On 2 May, under Billik's leadership, he scored his first victory when he downed the Camel of 2Lt H C Hickey of No 46 Sqn, which fell near Locon.

Billik apparently knew how to maximise the limited potential of the Pfalz D IIIa, and no doubt taught his pilots to do the same. On 3 May Billik got his third 'double', claiming a Camel at 1800 hrs and a Dolphin only 30 minutes later. His second victim was Capt G Chadwick, who came down wounded behind the German lines north of La Basée – the first Dolphin casualty for No 19 Sqn. Billik was on a hot streak, for six days later he shot down a No 2 Sqn Armstrong-Whitworth FK 8 in flames at Neuve Chapelle to bring his total to 16.

May provided other opportunities for pilots to claim their initial victims, for on the 17th Ltn d R Wilhelm Saint Mont and Gefr Marat

Schumm both received credit for SEs. Just before 1045 hrs, *Jasta* 52 was attacked by 'C' Flight from the renowned No 74 Sqn. 'Taffy' Jones related how Lt L M 'Nicky' Nixon had talked his way into going on his first flight over the lines with Flight Commander Capt W J Cairnes, and Jones lent Nixon his favourite aircraft and promised to keep an eye on the rookie. Over the lines the SEs dived on the *Jasta* 52 formation.

'The enemies were Pfalz scouts, well-flown and quite aggressive', wrote Jones. The Welsh ace fired a few bursts at a lone D IIIa and then zoomed up to let Nixon have a shot at it. 'When I had finished my zoom and had steadied myself to look for Nicky on the Hun's tail, I saw to my horror quite the reverse picture. The Hun was pumping lead into Nicky, who was diving in a straight line away from him. Before I could help, my dear old machine with my mascot and poor old Nicky was enveloped in flames. Why have we no parachutes, for God's sake?' Nixon was the first of Schumm's four victims.

Two days later Billik accounted for noted British ace Maj A D Carter DSO and Bar. A patrol of 13 Dolphins from No 19 Sqn had dived on a group of nine *Jasta* 52 Pfalz which were escorting a pair of two-seaters. Flight Commander Carter went for the two-seaters, but for some reason his Dolphin was seen to drop away. Swiftly Billik and a comrade swooped on the 28-victory Canadian and brought him down at 1110 hrs to spend the remainder of the war in a PoW camp. On 28 May Billik flamed an SE 5 from No 64 Sqn over Locon to bring his score to18.

Jasta 52 met their old foes from No 74 Sqn, led by 'Mick' Mannock, again on 1 June. 'Taffy' Jones recalled;

'The fight with Mick in the afternoon turned out to be the hottest dogfight I've been in for a few days. Mick led "A" and "C" Flights onto seven Pfalz Scouts, camouflaged dark, with white tails. It was cloudless where we fought over Estaires, between 4.25 and 4.35 pm at 13,000 ft. For ten minutes the ten SEs engaged the seven Pfalz, and when the battle ended one enemy had gone down in flames, one had crashed and one had gone out of control – all to Mick's guns – while we had lost our flight commander (the five-victory ace W J Cairnes). A determined Pfalz got to within 25 yards of him and gave him the gun. His right wing was suddenly seen to break up, the nose of his SE dipped viciously, then downwards he spun at a terrific rate.'

The 'determined Pfalz' was flown by Billik, who was lightly wounded in this scrap but returned safely and remained at the front. *Jasta* 52 lost Wilhelm Saint Mont to Mannock's deadly aim, the German jumping from his flaming Pfalz with a parachute but it tore and he fell to his death. There were no other German casualties.

On 5 June the *Staffel* joined with *Jasta* 22 in an attack on Bristols from No 20 Sqn that were on a bombing raid to Armentieres. Two F 2Bs from the rear of the formation were brought down and captured. They were credited to Juhnke (his third) and to Vfw Paul Reimann, but the latter pilot collided with one of the Bristols in the fight and crashed fatally. Nineteen days later Billik overcame another Bristol (from No 62 Sqn) for his significant 20th victory, putting him in line for the *Pour le Mérite*.

Evidence indicates that *Jasta* 52 finally obtained D VIIs – and some Fokker Dr Is – in late June or early July. Billik would receive his overdue 'Hohenzollern' on 25 July. He brought his total to an impressive 31 on

9 August, but the following day his D VII came down due to engine trouble and he was captured. In an unjust twist of fate, Billik's captivity would prevent his award of the 'Blue Max'.

Jasta 29

Another 6. *Armee* unit that flew the Pfalz D III and D IIIa was *Jasta* 29, which would serve in *Jagdgruppe* 7 along with *Staffeln* 30 and 52. *Jasta* 29 utilised a large percentage of Pfalz, but flew some Albatros fighters at the same time. In mid-December 1917 *Jasta* 29 was stationed at Bellinchamps airfield, and on the 28th Vfw Max Brandenburg was brought down by flak near Le Transloy to be taken prisoner in Pfalz D III 4020/17. The Pfalz was given the British code 'G 116', and had the rear fuselage and uppersurfaces of both wings painted dark green, while the undersides remained silver.

Jasta 29's leading light at this time was its commander, Oblt Harald Auffarth, who would survive the war with 29 successful claims. He may well have flown Pfalz fighters to achieve some of his seven or so victories from November 1917 through March 1918.

Karl Pech definitely did fly a Pfalz D IIIa to down some – if not all – of his nine opponents claimed in a meteoric blitz between March and May 1918. Born in Seidau on 9 December 1894, Pech came from *Jastaschule* I to the *Staffel* on 18 January 1918 as a lowly flieger. He wasted little time in proving his mettle, claiming a DH 4 on 13 March, and was soon promoted to unteroffizier. Pech followed this up with a Camel on the 27th and another victory on 22 April, and more came in rapid succession.

On the evening of 11 May he attained his sixth success when *Jasta* 29 attacked a formation of No 4 Sqn AFC Camels that were escorting a bombing raid on Armentières. Pech shot down the Sopwith of Lt O C Barry, 'whose machine fell in flames from a fierce duel' according to the official Australian history. On 18 May Pech subtracted a pair of Camels from the inventory of No 210 Sqn, and earned a promotion to vizefeldwebel.

The next day Pech was one of nine *Jasta* 29 pilots that encountered eight SE 5s from No 29 Sqn, led by 20-year-old Flight Commander Capt Hugh G White. In later years White wrote to Norman Franks;

'The incident occurred when we were shooting up a line of observation balloons, and that having seen the nine enemy Pfalz scouts approaching from above and my chaps having failed to react to my recall red Very Light signal, I decided to engage the nine in the hope of keeping them occupied until the rest of the formation followed on and joined in.'

White's CO, Maj Dixon, picks up the tale;

'Capt White was left alone. He dived on one of the EA (Pech's D IIIa) and fired about 100 rounds at very close range. The EA zoomed to the left and its top plane caught the leading edge of Capt White's machine, causing the EA to turn a

Vfw Karl Pech strikes a jaunty pose with his *Jasta* 29 Pfalz D IIIa. Like other aircraft of *Staffel* 29 at this period, this D IIIa was probably painted dark green on all uppersurfaces of the fuselage, tail, and wings – the spinner and cowling 'ring' just aft of it *may* have been yellow, which was part of the *Jasta* markings recorded later in 1918. It will be noted that two black(?) stripes appear on the *silbergrau* underside of the fuselage. The lower wing obscures an unidentifiable white personal marking on the fuselage. In the spring of 1918 Pech claimed nine opponents in a rapid-fire victory streak which came to an abrupt end on 19 May. On that day his Pfalz collided with SE 5a D3942 of Capt Hugh G White of No 29 Sqn and Pech was killed when the right wing of his machine tore away (*courtesy M Thiemeyer*)

cartwheel over his (White's) machine. The shock of the collision flung Capt White forward onto the gun mounting and stopped his engine. The EA went down in a dive and Capt White – expecting his machine to break up at any moment – dived after it, firing about 100 rounds. The right wing of the EA fell off, and it went down completely out of control. Capt White then turned round and headed west to endeavour to cross the lines.

'He was followed back by five EA scouts for some distance. Capt White managed to keep his machine fairly straight by putting on hard left bank, left rudder and leaning over the side of the cockpit. Near the ground, the machine became uncontrollable and crashed on landing near Eecke.'

White survived the crash to be credited with the D IIIa for his seventh victory. He was posted home three days later for a well-deserved rest. Pech was not as lucky, and is buried in the Lambersart German cemetery.

Jasta 30

Along with *Jasta* 10 of JG I, *Jasta* 30 is often considered the quintessential Pfalz *Staffel*. Unlike other nomadic units, *Jasta* 30 remained at Phalempin airfield in the 6. *Armee* for nearly its entire combat career. By the time the first Pfalz D III was delivered to the *Jasta* in October 1917, the unit had amassed a respectable 30 victories, and established a proud *esprit de corps*. From October 1917 through to February 1918, a mix of Pfalz and Albatros D V machines was flown, but from February to July 1918 the *Staffel* was solely equipped with the D IIIa.

The *Staffelführer* for the unit's first 14 months was the respected Oblt Hans Bethge. Born in Berlin on 6 December 1890, he enlisted as a fahnenjunker in *Eisenbahnregiment* 1 in Berlin-Schöneberg and was commissioned in 1912. After considerable service and a wound sustained on the Western Front, Bethge transferred to aviation. He flew with the famous bomber unit code-named *Brieftauben-Abteilung Ostende* (carrier pigeon unit Ostende) and its successor formation *Kampfgeschwader* 1.

Bethge was then posted to the single-seater unit *Kampfeinsitzerstaffel B* (for Bertincourt) on 4 August 1916 and flew Fokker Eindeckers with that group. He became a charter member of *Jasta* 1 on 22 August, and scored his first three victories there. Bethge was then assigned to take over the newly-formed *Jasta* 30 in January 1917, and he duly led the unit capably and was a steady, if not spectacular, scorer. By the time the first Pfalz

Twenty-seven-year-old Oblt Hans Bethge led *Jasta* 30 for 14 months after its creation in January 1917, and attained 17 of his 20 victories with the unit. *Jasta* 30 was based at Phalempin airfield for a lengthy period, and Bethge fostered a strong pride within the *Staffel* by the décor of its aircraft – and its hangars! The wooden hangars and the unit's 'ready shack' were adored with the rudders of downed Allied aircraft that served as colourful wind vanes. Here, Bethge poses on top of one of the hangars with a SPAD VII rudder. Just beyond him is the rudder from FE 8 A4887, flown by 2Lt P C S O'Longan of No 42 Sqn. Bethge shot down this FE 8 northeast of Warneton on 1 June 1917 for his seventh claim – O'Longan was killed (*A Imrie*)

Pilots of *Jasta* 30 relax at their stylish 'readiness hut' at Phalempin, in a view which emphasises the *esprit de corps* of this unit. Oblt Bethge is fifth from left, with an open book and a white scarf around his neck. Note the wind vane rudder on the roof – this came from FE 2d A6446 of No 20 Sqn RFC. This machine had been shot down by *Jasta* 30 ace Ltn Joachim von Bertrab on 15 May 1917 for his fifth victory, and the crew of 2Lt E J Grout and 2AM A R Tyrell were both taken PoW (*A Imrie*)

Pfalz D IIIa 5983/17 was the mount of Oblt Hans-Joachim Buddecke during his brief stay with *Jasta* 30 in February 1918. Buddecke was a celebrated *Pour le Mérite* winner who had first gained notoriety when he served as a Fokker Eindecker pilot over the Dardanelles, on the Turkish front. He had returned to the Western Front from his second tour of duty in Turkey in February 1918 – he may have been in some disgrace at this point, as he had earned notoriety of a different sort as an addicted gambler in Turkey. Buddecke gained his 13th, and final, victory in *Jasta* 30 on 19 February when he was credited with a Camel. The ace's Pfalz displayed only a stylised personal insignia (intended as a heart?) painted around the national insignia on the fuselage, and did not as yet show the unit's famed diamond emblem

It was a cold winter's day at Phalempin when these *Jasta* 30 pilots were photographed with a Pfalz D IIIa (possibly 4203/17). They are, from left to right, Ltn d R Hans Holthusen (four victories), Ltn von der Marwitz, Oblt Bethge (facing camera, hands in pockets), possibly Ltn Karl Weltz and Ltn Rudolf Freiherr von der Horst (facing camera). The warmly clothed groundcrew appear to be working on the Mercedes engine of the Pfalz (*A Imrie*)

arrived at Phalempin in October his tally stood at 17.

Bethge's pilots achieved a notable double victory on 3 January when they jumped a group of Camels from 'B' and 'C' Flights of the famed No 10 Naval Squadron, conspicuous in their brightly striped cowlings. The Sopwiths were attacking a German two-seater when *Jasta* 30 came to the rescue. Vfw Hans Oberländer 'made ace' when he forced down Flt Sub-Lt Beattie in Camel N6531, wounding him in the ankle. Beattie sat out the rest of the war as a PoW. Flt Sub-Lt Booth was not so lucky, as he was killed by Uffz Emil Liebert. Ironically Liebert was to perish later that same day when his aircraft struck a German balloon cable.

Oblt Hans-Joachim Buddecke was a highly decorated ace who briefly passed through the ranks of *Jasta* 30. A famous name from the heady days of the 'Fokker Scourge', Buddecke scored his initial victory in F. Fl. Abt. 23 on 23 October 1915. In December he was transferred to Turkey, where his exploits as a Fokker *Flieger* earned him only the third *Pour le Mérite* ever awarded to an airman. Buddecke returned to the Western Front to command *Jasta* 4 in August 1916, then was transferred back to Turkey, where he scored twice more on 30 March 1917. In February 1918 Buddecke once again returned to France, and was assigned to *Jasta* 30.

On 19 February, Bethge led his *Jasta* 30 Pfalz pilots into a scrap with Camels from No 80 Sqn northeast of Lens at 1405 hrs – the RFC unit had only arrived in France about three weeks earlier. Bethge, Buddecke and Ltn Hans-Georg von der Marwitz all achieved confirmed claims over the Sopwith rookies, two Camels being destroyed and a third pilot wounded, although he made it back across the lines. It was the 19th victory for Bethge, the third for von der Marwitz and the 13th (and last) for Buddecke.

On 8 March Buddecke's old friend Rudolf Berthold asked him to transfer to his *Jasta* 18 and help lead it, as Berthold was still in recovery

Eventually the Pfalz D IIIas of *Jasta* 30 would all boast the *Staffel's* unique black-bordered orange diamond marking. This was applied to both sides of the fuselage, both surfaces of the tailplane/elevator and to the centre section of the top wing as well. Seen here is D IIIa 4203/17 flown by Ltn Hans-Georg von der Marwitz, who would down 14 or 15 opponents and rise to command of the *Jasta*. Von der Marwitz personalised his Pfalz by having the orange unit colour extended to the fin and rudder, as well as to the diamond that graced the horizontal tail surfaces. This photograph was probably taken at Phalempin some time prior to the introduction of *Balkenkreuz* insignia in late March 1918

from a severe wound to his right arm. Two days later Buddecke was killed in combat with Camels from No 3 Naval Squadron.

The other victor on 19 February was the tall and aristocratic Hans-Georg von der Marwitz, the scion of an old and respected family. Born in Ohlau, Silesia, on 7 August 1893, he was the son of *General der Kavallerie* Georg von der Marwitz, the commander-in-chief of the entire German 2. *Armee.*

Initially a cavalryman like his father, Hans-Georg first served in *Ulanen Regt* Nr 16. In 1915-16 he was a member of *Infanterie Regt* Nr 13 and later 16, transferring to the *Fliegertruppe* in March. He flew with KG 5 and then *Schusta* 10, downing a Farman whilst flying with the latter unit for his first victory. Von der Marwitz trained as a fighter pilot in March and was posted to *Jasta* 30 on 18 April 1917. Less than a month later he torched a balloon west of Dixmude for his second kill, but then had a long dry stretch. A Camel claimed on 22 January went instead to a *Jasta* 26 pilot, but he finally garnered his third against No 80 Sqn.

10 March saw the *Staffelführer* down his 20th, and final, opponent – a DH 4 from No 18 Sqn that was shot down at Allennes at 1210 hrs. This victory brought Bethge a proposal for the 'Blue Max'. Six days later von der Marwitz, his dry spell clearly broken, gained his fourth with an FK 8.

On 17 March Bethge and five *Jasta* 30 airmen attacked a group of No 57 Sqn DH 4s that had just bombed Linselles. Bethge went for the de Havilland piloted by the veteran Capt A Roulstone, with observer 2Lt W Venmore. The RFC pilot pulled his DH 4 into an Immelmann and turned the tables on his foe, pumping 50 rounds into the Pfalz before his Vickers jammed. Roulstone then skilfully swung the big bomber around, allowing his observer to send 150 more bullets into the fighter, which went down trailing a dense cloud of smoke. Bethge was killed in Pfalz D IIIa 5888/17, his death precluding the award of the *Pour le Mérite.*

An unidentified *Jasta* 30 pilot plays with his dog in front of a highly decorated Pfalz D IIIa at Phalempin in February 1918. A variety of stripe patterns and colours were employed as personal insignia on *Jasta* 30 Pfalz, but they were not allowed to interfere with the orange diamond *Staffel* marking (*A Imrie*)

On 30 March the *Staffel* suffered another casualty when Uffz Marczinke was taken PoW in Pfalz D IIIa 8278/18, a victim of flak. Von der Marwitz must have improved the morale of the *Jasta* on 12 April when he shot down a brace of the

A busy day at Phalempin finds a pilot cavorting with his canine friend as three well-decorated Pfalz have been set up in flying positions on trestles. The D IIIa at right boasts a coloured fin as a personal emblem, while the other two display striped markings. Once again the unique wind vanes on the hangar roof may be noted, with the rudder from FE 8 A4887 (Bethge's seventh victim) showing up prominently (*Katzenstein album/A Imrie*)

A group of happy *Jasta* 30 pilots cluster about one of their D IIIa fighters on Phalempin. They are, from left to right, Uffz Josef Funk (3 victories), Ltn Erich Kaus, Ltn d R Reinhold Maier (2), Ltn Hans Eggers, Ltn d R Hans Oberländer (6), Ltn Ewald Siempelkamp (OzbV, with arms akimbo and dark trousers), Ltn von der Marwitz (with back to camera, holding up walking stick) and a little-known pilot named Ltn Konig. The Pfalz had five-colour printed fabric on the wings and tailplane, and on the original photo the orange diamond emblem can just be made out on these components. The unknown pilot's personal marking consisted of the slightly slanted dark stripes painted on the otherwise silver-grey fuselage. The method of converting the wing crosses to the current form of *Balkenkreuz* may be noted (*A Imrie*)

vaunted Sopwith Camels. At 0830 hrs he destroyed a machine of No 54 Sqn, killing Lt J R Sandford. Three hours later he added Camel D1850 of No 73 Sqn, ending the life of 2Lt M F Korslund. Four days later von der Marwitz took command of the *Jasta*. Yet another Camel fell to the nobleman's guns on 16 May when Lt W E Cowan of No 208 Sqn was forced down at Lorgies.

May was an eventful month for the rest of the *Staffel* as well. Oberländer destroyed a No 40 Sqn SE 5 on the 20th for his sixth score, but was wounded three days later and left the unit. Hans Holthusen

RAF pilot Lt W E Cowan of No 208 Sqn (left) seems quite relieved and happy to pose with his captor, Ltn Hans-Georg von der Marwitz. Now the commander of *Jasta* 30 after Bethge's death, von der Marwitz shot down Cowan's Camel D9540 near Lorgies at 0740 hrs on 16 May 1918. The D IIIa in the background was the machine von der Marwitz flew as *Staffelführer,* and according to two sources it was apparently painted in a dark 'wine red' or burgundy colour over the fuselage and upper wing surfaces. The spinner and metal cowling panels were left unpainted – note the unusual windscreen. The *Staffel* emblem of the orange diamond can just be seen behind von der Marwitz (*information and photo A Imrie, additional info M Thiemeyer*)

This view of *Jasta* 30 pilot Ltn Erich Kaus provides a fine look at the *Staffel* marking as applied to his Pfalz D IIIa. Kaus was posted to the unit from *Armee Flug Park* 6 on 2 December 1917, and flew with *Jasta* 30 until he was wounded in combat with SE 5s on 31 May 1918. While other pilots had trouble recovering from a flat spin in a Pfalz, Kaus apparently did not. When interviewed by Alex Imrie, he stated that he personally liked the Pfalz D IIIa very much, and that his favourite method of losing height was to spin down over the airfield (*A Imrie*)

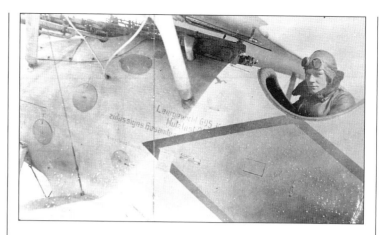

Pfalz D IIIa 8233/17 bore a beautifully striped fuselage in addition to the *Staffel* diamond insignia. When photographed here with *Balkenkreuz* insignia, this Pfalz was the machine of Ltn Erich Kaus. However, there is circumstantial evidence that this machine was previously flown by *Staffelführer* Hans Bethge, when it would have displayed iron cross markings. In *Jasta* 30 pilot Otto Fuchs' fictionalised account of the unit, the Bethge character is described as having an aircraft with longitudinal grey and white stripes, like a 'flying trout'. Some historians have opined, therefore, that Bethge must also have flown this Pfalz D IIIa at one time. Bethge was killed flying Pfalz 5888/17, thus 8223/17 might then have been passed on to Kaus. This machine had five-colour printed camouflage fabric on the wings, and the *Jasta* marking can be seen on the fuselage, tail and upper wing centre section. Note the rack of flare cartridges next to the cockpit and the ASI on the starboard strut (*A Imrie*)

achieved the first of his two victories on the 21st, but Vfw Schiebler was killed in his Pfalz on the 27th. Four days later Ltn Erich Kaus was also wounded.

On 9 June *Jasta* 30 was again victorious over No 210 Sqn Camels as von der Marwitz led his Pfalz pilots into a scrap over Ploegstreet Wood. Lt Marsden became the second airman from his squadron to be taken

Ltn Kaus' spectacularly decorated D IIIa 8233/17 continues to undergo maintenance at Phalempin. The wheel hubs may have been covered with 'lozenge' fabric, then thinly overpainted in the field (*A Imrie*)

prisoner by the *Staffelführer,* and Ltn d R Kurt Katzenstein forced down Lt Breckenbridge for his sole victory. Katzenstein survived the conflict to become a respected aerobatic and racing pilot in the interwar years. Together with another Jewish ex-fighter pilot, Anton 'Toni' Raab of *Jasta* 40, he founded an aircraft manufacturing enterprise known as Raab-Katzenstein Flugzeugwerke GmbH in 1925, which had two associated flying schools. Due to the rising anti-Semitism in Germany, both Raab and Katzenstein left the country in 1931.

At some time around July 1918 *Jasta* 30 said farewell to its faithful Pfalz machines as D VIIs started to arrive. Von der Marwitz was wounded on 17 June, but returned on 1 August to command the unit to war's end – by then he had 14 or 15 victories. Von der Marwitz would subsequently be killed in a fiery aircraft crash on 12 May 1925.

Jasta 21s

Jagdstaffel 21 had achieved an enviable reputation on the French front under the leadership of the Bavarian ace Eduard Schleich. By late October 1917 – about the time when the first Pfalz began to arrive – the *Staffel* had amassed an impressive total of 59 victories. Besides Schleich, one of its top aces was Ltn d R Emil Thuy with a score of 15 – on 29 September he left to command *Jasta* 28. On 21 October Schleich was unceremoniously relieved of his office and sent to command the Bavarian *Jasta* 32. His place was taken by Oblt Oskar Freiherr von Boenigk, who had flown the Pfalz D III in *Jasta* 4.

Ironically, on 25 October *Jasta* 21 was designated a Saxon unit, but it retained its proud unit marking of two fuselage stripes in Prussian black and white to war's end.

It is believed that the *Jasta* introduced the use of the Pfalz in the 5. *Armee,* but the unit probably never had a full complement of D IIIs or D IIIas. One Pfalz flier was the 'balloon buster' Ltn d R Fritz Höhn. A native of Wiesbaden, the 21-year-old Höhn had served in the elite 7th Guards Infantry Regiment before joining the *Fliegertruppe*. Having flown two-seaters in Fl. Abt. (A) 227 before switching to fighters, he came to *Staffel* 21 from *Jastaschule* II on 15 November 1917 when the unit was at Villers la Chèvre, in the 5. *Armee*. Höhn's first victory came promptly 16 days later when he received credit for a French bomber southwest of Chattencourt.

He was apparently beginning to plan a campaign against French kite balloons, and had his Pfalz D III 4011/17 painted in 'dazzle' stripes to break up the outline of the aeroplane. However, Höhn was unsuccessful in his chosen specialty until 11 April 1918, by which time he was probably flying a D IIIa. On that date he claimed to have attacked two gasbags over Brimont, although those claims were discounted – a

One of the most notable aces of *Jasta* 21s was Ltn d R Emil Thuy, who chalked up 15 of his eventual 35 victories with the unit. On 29 September 1917, Thuy was posted out of *Jasta* 21s to take command of Royal Württemberg *Jasta* 28, where this photograph was taken. Thuy is seated in Pfalz D III 4017/17 in November 1917, probably at Varsenare, near Brügge. The Pfalz appears new and pristine, and it has been fitted with a tubular gunsight. Thuy would lead the *Jasta* to war's end, and earn the *Pour le Mérite (A Imrie)*

third attack on the balloon of the 33e *Compagnie de Aérostiers* ignited it for his second confirmed victory. He followed that up the next day with a SPAD for his third.

On 20 April Höhn resumed his balloon hunting and burnt a brace of French gasbags, one each from the 45e and 75e *Compagnies*. His double cost him dearly, for he received a severe knee wound on this sortie that sidelined him for four months. Returning to *Jasta* 21s on 16 August, and probably flying a D VII, in four days he picked up where he left off with another balloon for his seventh victory. A Breguet and a SPAD were also quickly despatched. Höhn was successively posted to *Jasta* 81 and *Jasta* 60 as acting commander of each unit, adding eight more to his tally (four of them balloons). On 1 October he was placed in full command of *Jasta* 41, where he added three more for a final total of 21 before he was killed in combat on 3 October 1918.

One other *Jasta* 21s Pfalz pilot who succumbed to 'balloon fever' was Ltn Busso von Alvensleben. He was born in Wittenmoor on 21 April 1898. After serving as a pilot in *Kampfstaffel* 19 of *Kampfgeschwader* 4, he began his career as a fighter pilot in *Jasta* 4 of the Richthofen 'Circus' in July 1917. On 27 November 1917 he transferred to *Jasta* 21s. Von Alvensleben was still flying a Pfalz D IIIa in the summer of 1918, and in some ten months as a *Jagdflieger* he had failed to score a single victory. That changed on fateful 14 June, when he succeeded in flaming a balloon

of the 45e *Cie de Aérostiers* near Crépy-en-Valois. Tragically, he was wounded in the course of his attack and came down in Allied lines. He died as a prisoner the next day at Villers-Cotterets.

Jasta 61

Jagdstaffel 61 also flew the Pfalz D IIIa on the French sector. This unit was formed at *Flieger-Beobachter-Schule Köln* on 11 January 1918, and moved to the front on the 23rd under the command of Oblt Maximilian Edler von Daniels. It set up shop at Voyenne, near Marle in the 7. *Armee,* and would be entirely equipped with the Pfalz D IIIa.

The first pilot to arrive was the veteran Vfw Kurt Jentsch, the Pfalz Eindecker pilot featured in Chapter One. After his service in Macedonia (where he gained perhaps as many as three victories), Jentsch transferred to the Western Front. Flying with *Jasta* 1 in June 1917, he was credited with a SPAD – his first officially recorded Western Front victory – on the 23rd. From August 1917 to January 1918, Jentsch flew as a Rumpler pilot in Fl. Abt. (A) 234, then returned to fighters in *Jasta* 61. He told the story of the unit's aircraft in *Jagdflieger im Feuer;*

'On 27 January, the aeroplanes finally arrive – Pfalz biplanes, model D IIIa, silver-grey aircraft.

'The commander instructed me to "break in" all of the aeroplanes, including testing the guns. In spite of the perils, I did all of them on 15 February. The birds are ready for take-off.

'Right from the beginning, this was a black day; our Special Duties Officer (Ltn d R Ferner) has crashed. During a practice bank, his Pfalz slipped away from him and smashed into the ground with the throttle full out. We could only recover the dead man from the tangle of splintered spars, rigging cables and fabric shreds. A rigging wire had cut through his skull.'

One of Jentsch's first sorties was almost his last;

'On 5 March at 2.15 in the afternoon, we went to the frontlines. The *Kette* was flying under my leadership. We kept a lookout for the French at all heights. Behind us, an unending series of shrapnel clouds stretched out. The French flak accompanied us from Berry au Bac to Chavignon. The altimeter read 4500 metres.

'On the other side, in the area of Soissons, I spotted two Breguet biplanes that had their eyes on our frontlines. After a quick consideration, I dive over our lines and tie myself on to one of the two Frenchmen. After a wild dogfight, during which I often got a shot in, he rushed downwards with fluttering wings. During the fight, which was in the end played out at 3500 metres, the flak guns were silent – now they flash like mad. In no time I'm sitting between bursting artillery and shrapnel shells. All hell has broken loose.

'I am just about to beat it in a dive when there is an explosion close by. A violent jolt goes through my aeroplane, and it shudders and shakes throughout the struts and frame – it is only thanks to the position I had already assumed for the dive that I do not crash downwards in a helpless spin. A shell explodes just under my aircraft and stifling smoke pours out into the fuselage, forcing me to cough. Standing on my nose, I now save myself from the flak fire. The plywood fairing (of the fuselage, beneath the cockpit) is ripped away by a shell – cold streams of air blow around my legs. I'm sitting there half freezing!

'While in the dive, I hit the throttle now and then, and the engine rages like crazy. It appears that a piece of the propeller has been shot off – that is why the engine is running this way. Quick as lightning, thoughts race through my head. "It's over – you're going to be a prisoner!" The earth approaches closer and closer, and with it my fate. I get a grip on myself. "Even if your aeroplane flies with all the shreds flapping about your ears, you still have to make it over and reach the German lines".

'At the height of 100 metres, smoke envelopes me – the outlook is abysmal. Carefully, I put the engine into gear. It runs with a clatter and is skipping like mad. The wings begin to dance and the struts play along. The entire aircraft is swerving as if it wants to break up at any moment. Through the hole in the plywood hull, I can see the ground over which I'm rushing. The undercarriage has gone to the devil, the direct hit ripping it away.

'The powerful air stream that is entering into the fuselage everywhere has ripped out the empty ammunition belts – they fly away to the right

Jagdstaffel 61 went into action in February 1918 equipped entirely with the Pfalz D IIIa. Seen here is Ltn d Landwehr Karl Becker of the *Jasta* in his D IIIa 6021/17, who seems well prepared for the freezing temperatures of high-altitude flight in an open cockpit. This view provides a good look at the weights table and other fuselage details. Becker was born on 7 March 1894, and flew with *Jasta* 61 for several months without obtaining a victory. He was shot down in flames by SPADs over Fretoy on 6 June 1918 (*HAC/UTD*)

The Pfalz D IIIa did not enjoy an auspicious start with *Jasta* 61. On 10 February the unit's OzbV (special duties officer) was killed in this crash at Voyenne. Kurt Jentsch recalled that the Pfalz 'slipped away from him' during a bank in a practice flight. A rigging cable cut through Ferner's skull. The serial number of this D IIIa is visible at the top of the rudder, and appears to have been 6015/17, although *Jasta* records give the number 6013/17 (*R Kastner*)

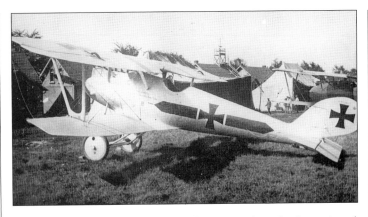

One Pfalz-equipped *Staffel* which served on the French front in the 7. *Armee* along with *Jasta* 61 was Royal Saxon *Jasta* 22. This unit was commanded by ace Ltn d R Alfred Lenz from July 1917 to the armistice, and operated a mix of Pfalz and Albatros for some time. This photograph was reportedly taken at Mont airfield, near Verdun in the 5. *Armee*, which was occupied by *Jasta* 22s from mid-August to mid-October 1917. Pfalz D III 1386/17 was flown by Lenz, as was the dark-painted Albatros D V in the background. The markings on the fuselage, upper wing and tail were black, and were entirely personal insignia. It seems unlikely that any of Lenz' six confirmed claims were scored in this machine. By the war's final day Lenz had served at the front for 42 months, and built up more than 800 flying hours *(A Imrie)*

and left as narrow bands, many metres long. Everything that is not riveted or nailed down comes off and goes overboard. The machine gun covering leaps away and falls into the depths. It can only be a matter of minutes before the rest breaks up into thin air.

'If I can yet make it to the canal behind Chavignon, I'll be all right. How I am to land this flying coffin is still a mystery to me. Everything that is bolted on now flashes out of the living corpse. The wings have been holed like a colander – I dare not bank because of the danger of them breaking. The engine is shaking about. It is only hanging by the fuel lines. Because of this I can only accept "the blessings" (the enemy's fire) which come from below.

'Right in front of the canal they place a second direct hit into my aircraft. A black cloud of smoke blocks my view – the engine has stopped running. The riddled tanks spurt fuel and oil in fountains due to the pressure. Half blinded, I yank the ignition out and put the Pfalz on its nose. Smoking, the flying coffin – the controls still responding – roars down on to the shell craters near the canal!

'I know that I instinctively did a loop and fell into a large shell crater on my back. I hit my head on something. Little stars appear from the direction of the sky, then I lose consciousness.'

After he came to, Jentsch managed to crawl to the German trenches, where he was taken in by some Bavarian troops. He was soon able to report back to his CO, who had given him up for dead.

Around the end of March, *Jasta* 61 was re-equipped with Albatros D Vas. In mid-July the unit was allotted Pfalz D XII fighters, and Fokker D VIIs arrived by the end of the month. On 13 August Jentsch finally

For the latter part of April 1918, *Jagdstaffeln* 61 and 22s were both operating in the 18. *Armee* sector near St Quentin. Another unit in the same *Armee* was Royal Saxon *Jasta* 72, informally known as '*Jagdstaffel* Menckhoff' after its renowned commander Ltn d R Carl Menckhoff. This rare view shows a line-up of *Jasta* 72s Pfalz and Albatros, but the pilot of the striped D IIIa in the foreground is unknown. At least some of the unit's Albatros aircraft were similarly striped. Since the *Jasta* was a Saxon unit, it is very likely the Albatros were striped in Saxon green and white, with a green nose. The foremost Pfalz seen here was probably also decorated in green, although the basic *silbergrau* finish of the fuselage sufficed in place of white. The fin and rudder were probably white and the wings seem to have been covered in five-colour 'lozenge' fabric *(photo courtesy J Leckscheid, information from M Thiemeyer)*

The Albatros and Pfalz aircraft of *Kampfeinsitzerstaffel (Kest)* 8w were decorated with a writhing snake coiled around the fuselage, with the head and tail always turning up on the port side. Four jaunty comrades of *Kest* 8 were photographed riding the fuselage of Vfw Carl Bücker's Pfalz D IIIa 4229/17. They are, from left to right, Uffz Willy Neuenhofen, Off Stv Franz Hilger, Bücker and Offz Stv Paul Bohlen. Bücker is thought to have downed opponents on both the Eastern and Western Fronts for a total of three victories, although he never flew in a *Jasta*

obtained a coveted posting to *Jasta* Boelcke, but he received a wound on 4 September that ended his war.

Kest 8w

Some Pfalz D III and D IIIa machines were to be found in the home defence fighter units known as the *Kampfeinsitzer Staffeln*. These units garnered relatively few victories and fewer aces, but at least one successful *Kest* pilot flew the Pfalz in *Kest* 8w.

Carl Bücker achieved the rare distinction of scoring victories on both the Eastern and Western Fronts, yet never served in a *Jasta*. Born on 21 June 1892 near Osnabrück, he managed to obtain a posting to Fl. Abt. (A) 230 in June 1916 after being a flight instructor. This unit flew in support of the Austrian army in Galicia. Besides the usual two-seaters, the *Abteilung* also had two Roland D II scouts on strength for occasional fighter sorties.

It was on one such mission that Bücker flamed a Russian balloon around June 1917 for his first confirmed victory. On New Year's Day 1918 he arrived at *Kest* 8w on the Western Front, apparently in the 4. *Armee*. There, Bücker flew both D III and D IIIa machines, adorned with the distinctive spiral snake marking of the *Kest*. He was transferred to *Kest* 1a at Mannheim on 17 May, and on 16 August he downed his second confirmed opponent, a DH 4 over Buchsweiler. From 20 August to the end of the war, Vfw Bücker flew with *Kest* 7. He apparently obtained his third victory with that unit some time in October 1918.

Bücker remained active in aviation in the 1920s and 30s. During World War 2 he was recalled to active duty in the Luftwaffe and trained glider pilots, rising to the rank of hauptmann. He died on 5 October 1970.

Pfalz D IIIa and Albatros fighters of *Kest* 8w show off their elaborate markings in this unique line-up shot. The first aircraft is Bücker's D IIIa 4229/17, while the second Pfalz is marked with a white snake insignia. The snake markings obviously varied in their hue, and in the number of coils wrapped around the fuselage. Some of the Albatros machines feature light-coloured serpents, while others are dark, but all seem to have their tails and noses painted a pale colour or colours

PFALZ D VIII AND D XII

The history of the Pfalz fighters and the aces that flew them does not end with the D IIIa. In January 1918 *Idflieg* conducted the First Fighter Competition at Adlershof, which saw test pilots and veteran frontline airmen flying various designs from different firms. The goal was to select the best of the new fighter prototypes. Pfalz submitted five different designs, among them the compact D VIII biplane powered by the 160 hp Siemens-Halske Sh III counter-rotary.

The D VIII was selected for limited production, and 120 examples of the fast-climbing interceptor aircraft were ordered. Some of these would serve in the home-defence *Kests*.

In March 1918 *Idflieg* ordered the D XII into production as well. It was usually powered by the Mercedes D IIIaü and fitted with a SPAD type twin-bay wing cellule. Approximately 750 Pfalz D XII fighters would be built.

PFALZ D VIII

Although a mere 14 Pfalz D VIII machines were recorded at the front on 30 June 1918 and 19 were inventoried two months later, photographs have survived showing three of these were flown by aces, at least nominally. Whether or not many confirmed victories were scored on the D VIII is another matter.

Without doubt the most celebrated of all Pfalz D VIII exponents was Ltn d R Paul Wilhelm Bäumer, who would survive the war with 43 confirmed victories. Born in Duisberg on 11 May 1896, Bäumer served as a dental apprentice in the pre-war years, but satisfied his burning desire to fly by taking pilot's instruction.

When war broke out he volunteered with *Infanterie Regt* Nr 70, seeing action on both Western and Eastern Fronts. Following a wound, Bäumer managed to talk his way into the *Fliegertruppe* and flew the Rumpler C IV in Fl. Abt. 7 in 1917. After fighter instruction, he was posted briefly to *Jasta* 5, scoring three victories there before being posted to *Jasta* 'Boelcke' on 15 August. Flying Albatros and Fokker Dr I fighters with *Jasta* 'B', he speedily increased his tally. On 12 February 1918 he was awarded the *Militär Verdienst Kreuz* and on 23 March he achieved a 'triple' to bring his total to 22. Bäumer was finally commissioned on 10 April.

Ltn d R Paul Bäumer's Pfalz D VIII boasted full unit and personal markings by the time this photograph was taken. The original fully-bordered *Balkenkreuz* insignia on the grey fuselage were carefully overpainted so they would not conflict with the pilot's individual emblem of the red-white-black chevron – the overpainted cross can just be seen. The national insignia was updated to the latest style and repainted further aft. The rear fuselage and empennage were decorated in the well-known *Jasta* 'Boelcke' marking of a half-white, half-black tail (although the former colour looks more off-white when compared to the rudder). The rudder was white on both sides, while the wings were covered in five-colour printed fabric (*A Imrie*)

This frontal view of Bäumer's Pfalz D VIII reveals details of the large propeller and the painting of the cowling in *Jasta* 'Boelcke' black and white. The oil spewed out through the cooling holes in the cowling points to some engine trouble. The four-bladed propeller was made up of two regular props bolted together – a measure that saved time and shipping space, but which may have led to a slight weight increase. Bäumer may not have had too many opportunities to fly this machine in combat (*A Imrie*)

Paul Bäumer strikes a relaxed pose with his cigar and Pfalz D VIII. He suffered severe jaw injuries in a crash on 29 May, most likely in this machine. Bäumer would not receive his well-earned 'Blue Max' until 2 November 1918, by which time he had attained all of his 43 victories

It is believed that Bäumer obtained his unique Pfalz D VIII (possibly 124/18) at some point in mid to late May 1918. This was likely the only D VIII allotted to *Jasta* 'Boelcke', and it may be indicative of Bäumer's status as one of the leading lights of an elite *Jasta* that he was able to procure one of the new interceptors for frontline assessment. Reportedly, Bäumer preferred the nimble flying qualities offered by a rotary-engined aeroplane to those of a stationary-engined machine. Now that JG III was beginning to relinquish its Fokker Dr Is for D VIIs, he may have felt the D VIII was a fitting replacement for his triplane.

At any rate, Bäumer's D VIII was soon painted up in *Jasta* 'Boelcke' colours and decorated with his personal red-white-black chevron stripes on the fuselage. However, he did not have much time to fly it, and did not attain any victories with the scout. Bäumer flew it with great dexterity, however. His friend Joachim von Hippel told Alex Imrie that, 'Later, when Bäumer used to visit *Jasta* 5 at Boistrancourt in his Pfalz and Fokker aircraft from *Jasta* "Boelcke", he normally ran his undercarriage wheels on the hangar roof to get the wheels revolving before touching down!'

On 21 May JG III was transferred to Vivaise on the 7. *Armee* front to support the German offensive on the Aisne. On 29 May Bäumer was returning to the airfield from a flight at about 2230 hrs. In the fading light of dusk he misjudged his landing and crashed badly, sustaining a complex fracture of the lower jaw. He was out of action for over three months.

When Bäumer finally returned to *Jasta* 'B' in September, he soon made up for lost time. He added 16 aircraft to his record by the end of the month and five more in October – no doubt while flying a Fokker D VII. The *Pour le Mérite* finally came on 2 November, and he finished the war performing special duties testing new fighter types at Adlershof. Bäumer was killed on 15 July 1927 when the Rohrbach Rofix fighter he was test-flying crashed near Copenhagen.

One *Staffel* which received the D VIII in some quantity was *Jasta* 29. The *Staffelführer* was still Oblt Harald Auffarth, who was photographed with a D VIII and probably flew it in combat. Auffarth had first flown two-seaters in Fl. Abt. (A) 266, then did his initial stint as a *Jagdflieger* in *Jasta* 18 under Berthold in September 1917 – racking up five quick victories that same month.

On 20 October Bäumer's rapid success brought him the acting command of *Jasta* 29, which was made official on 19 November. He was wounded in the hand on 28 May but returned to his command on 21 June. His momentous 20th victory came on 3 September – the same day he took over leadership of *Jagdgruppe* 3 (comprised of *Jagdstaffeln* 14, 16b, 29 and 56). Records of Bäumer's final claims are somewhat fragmentary, although the *Heeresbericht* for 30 October 1918 mentioned his 29th and 30th victories.

An alternate form of four-bladed propeller is in use on this *Jasta* 29 Pfalz D VIII that was photographed with the *Staffelführer* Oblt Harald Auffarth. It is likely that this cowling was painted yellow as part of the *Staffel* décor and the rest of the fuselage was almost certainly dark green. If Auffarth did indeed have his own personal D VIII, one wonders if it might have borne a white comet emblem like that seen on his Fokker D VII (*HAC/UTD*)

His recommended *Pour le Mérite* never came through due to the Armistice, although he did receive the 'Hohenzollern' and both the Bremen and Hamburg Hanseatic Crosses.

Another noted *Jasta* 29 pilot who probably flew the D VIII was Karl Gregor. Transferring to the air service from the ground troops in May 1915, he performed exemplary service flying two-seaters with Fl. Abt. (A) 210 in 1916 and had one unconfirmed victory with the unit. Gregor joined *Jasta* 29 in late May 1917 and attained his first credited victory on 29 June. He was severely wounded in the left leg during a fierce dogfight over Dixmuiden on 27 July, and the injured limb was amputated at the thigh. After a lengthy hospital stay he was sent home with a 75 per cent pension on 31 May 1918.

Gregor was a determined sort, however, and he returned to flying fitted with prosthesis and rejoined his old *Staffel* on 1 July. In spite of his handicap, he downed an SE 5 on 22 July for his second kill and a DH 9 for number three on 8 August 1918. Propagandistic German accounts published in the 1930s claimed that Gregor had just landed on the *Jasta* 29 airfield near Péronne after this victory when another formation of RAF bombers appeared overhead to rain more destruction on the pockmarked field. Reportedly, while other *Staffel* pilots took off to intercept the British aircraft, Gregor stayed behind and manned a defensive ground machine gun – he is supposed to have shot down one or two of the bombers in this way, but this seems far-fetched.

The *Jasta* war diary gives Vfw Gregor credit for a fourth victory in October before he was relieved of his duties due to health problems with his leg stump and his heart. This stalwart airman was awarded the Golden Military Merit Cross on 30 October and made an officer the next day.

Along with *Jasta* 29, another unit in *Jagdgruppe* 3 in late 1918 was *Jasta* 56. Photographic evidence shows

The men of *Jasta* 29 are seen with two of the unit's Pfalz D VIII fighters. Second from left, his arms linked with two comrades, is Vfw Karl Gregor, who at this time was flying with a prosthetic left leg. Fifth from left is Oblt Harald Auffarth, the *Jasta* commander. Gregor did not arrive back at *Jasta* 29 until 1 July 1918, so this photograph must have been taken soon after his return. By 16 July the *Staffel* had some Fokker D VIIs on hand, for Vfw Wackwitz of the unit was killed in a crash of one on that date. It is possible the *Jasta* flew both Pfalz D VIII and Fokkers for a period. The two Pfalz seen here apparently bear the unit's dark green fuselage and light yellow cowlings, while a personal marking of a white fleur-de-lis can just be made out on the D VIII at left (*A Imrie*)

A grim-faced Ludwig 'Lutz' Beckmann of *Jasta* 56 is seen second from left with his Pfalz D VIII 178/18. Fourth from left is Uffz Ludwig Jeckert, who obtained four victories with the *Staffel*. The cowling and tail of the D VIII are clearly painted in *Staffel* colours. Whilst under the command of Ltn d R Collin, *Jasta* 56's aircraft were marked with a yellow nose and tail. Therefore, it is likely that this D VIII, and others in the unit, displayed a yellow cowling and tail section at some time. Beckmann told historian H J Nowarra that his own Fokker D VII had a red nose and tail, so it seems that the unit marking changed when he took over the *Staffel* in August 1918. The *Jasta's* markings then became a blue-grey fuselage and red nose and tail. As a Westphalian, Beckmann preferred red and white personal markings, so it may be that this D VIII went against the earlier *Staffel* policy and bore a red nose and tail

that Ltn d R Ludwig Beckmann of the *Jasta* flew Pfalz D VIII 178/18, at least for a while. 'Lutz' first flew fighters in *Jasta* 6 in December 1917, then went to *Jasta* 48 for a brief stint on 21 February 1918. On 10 March he transferred to *Jasta* 56, and achieved his first victory only three days later with an RE 8. A Camel was added to his score on 9 May, then a double on 22 July brought his tally to four. It is not recorded exactly when he flew the Pfalz D VIII, but the final half of his eight victories were probably accounted for in a Fokker. Beckmann commanded the *Jasta* from 15 August to the Armistice.

Under Ltn d R Diether Collin's command, the aircraft of the unit reportedly boasted yellow noses and tails, with 'blue-grey' fuselages added on their D VIIs. When Beckmann took over, he is said to have changed the yellow components to red. So, much hinges on when Beckmann flew a D VIII, and if his Westphalian roots caused him to go against *Staffel* policy to have the cowling and empennage of his D VIII painted red instead of yellow early on – either is possible. There were certainly some examples of the D VIII in *Jasta* 56 with yellow noses and tails.

PFALZ D XII

The frontline inventories show that five D XIIs had reached the rear-area *Armee Flugparks* or selected *Staffeln* by 30 June 1918. By the end of August this had risen to 168 machines. Many units received new Pfalz to augment their Fokker D VIIs and to replace the weary Albatros D Va and Pfalz D IIIa aeroplanes still in service.

The fuselage of a *Jasta* 43 Pfalz D XII is brought back to Haubourdin airfield, apparently after an accident wiped off its undercarriage. The aircraft most likely belonged to Gefr Walter Blumensaath, who is thought to be the pilot seen here in the cockpit. This photograph was taken on 16 July 1918, and Blumensaath had only arrived at the *Jasta* at the end of June. The pilots, from left to right, are Blumensaath (in cockpit), unknown, Vfw Ernst Wiehle (6 victories), Ltn d R Josef Raesch, Uffz Paul Rüggeberg, and Vfw Max Kiep (on fin, 3 victories, killed 3 October 1918). The D XII fuselage displayed a factory finish grey fuselage and the *Staffel* marking of a white tail, with a personal number '10' on the fin. Later this same day, the *Jasta* aerodrome at Haubourdin was bombed and strafed by British aircraft and Raesch's own Pfalz D XII went up in flames (*HAC/UTD*)

Jagdstaffel 17 also received some examples of the Pfalz D XII. The unknown pilot seen here chose to personalise his Pfalz with the name *Wildfang* painted in white on the grey fuselage, just visible aft of the cross. Loosely translated, *Wildfang* means 'an unruly child, a madcap, especially a tomboy'. The nose is painted in the dark *Staffel* colour, and a personal dark band was applied lengthwise along the grey fuselage. A tube for a flare pistol was mounted beside the cockpit (*HAC/UTD*)

Ltn d R Schulte-Schlutius (a former uhlan, judging from his uniform) poses with his highly painted Pfalz D XII of *Jasta* 3. The D XII apparently had the entire fuselage painted a dark colour, with a white nose. *Jasta* 3 was one of those *Staffeln* of the 19. *Armee* positioned to counter the raids of the Independent Air Force against industrial targets in southwestern Germany. On 7 September 1918, a raid on Mannheim by DH 9s of No 104 Sqn was intercepted by fighters from *Kest* 1a and *Jagdstaffeln* 80b and 3. Schulte-Schlutius received credit for his sole victory that day with a DH 9 downed at Buchsweiler. It was a disastrous day for No 104 Sqn, which lost seven aircraft crews either dead, wounded or PoW (*HAC/UTD*)

A few D XIIs were supplied to *Jasta* 43 in the 6. *Armee*. Ltn d R Josef Raesch was an experienced pilot who had flown the Albatros D Va and Fokker D VII with the unit for some time (he is variously credited with between three and seven victories). On 26 July he narrowly escaped incineration when he took to his parachute from a flaming D VII. After a two week leave he wrote in his diary;

'13 August 1918 – I have been issued a new aeroplane, but instead of being a Fokker D VII, the machine is a Pfalz D XII. It is alleged to be a fine aeroplane.

'14 August – A flight with the Pfalz does not satisfy me at all. The machine is clumsy in turns and does not climb well.

'15 August – After two more flights with the Pfalz D XII, I am very unhappy that I must fly it. The machine will not keep up with the others in formation.

'16 August – At 1000 hrs, we started on a sortie. Contrary to my first opinions, I get along well with my Pfalz when flying in formation. Around noon time we really had an experience. More than 80 hostile aircraft arrived above our aerodrome and, in spite of heavy flak fire, they dive-bombed us and fired incendiary ammunition at our hangars and aircraft. We ran out of our mess hall onto the field. Flames were everywhere. Two mechanics of our groundcrew were slightly injured. Three of our machines, Schobinger's, Rüggeberg's and my Pfalz D XII, were burning.'

The *Jasta* operations were severely hampered by a lack of machines for some time, but on 3 September six Fokkers finally arrived. Raesch never scored in his D XII.

Another unit to operate the D XII was Bavarian *Jasta* 35, under the command of Rudolf Stark. By September 1918 the *Staffel* had already acquired a few Fokker D VIIs, but still needed more. Stark wrote in *Der Jagdstaffel unsere Heimat*;

'1/9/18 – We are to have more new machines. Everyone is pleased, especially the pilots who have not yet got their Fokkers. But their joy is soon dampened, for the machines allotted to them are not Fokkers but Pfalz D XIIs.

In September 1918 *Jasta* 35b
reluctantly acquired several Pfalz
D XII fighters to augment their
Fokker D VIIs. One of the unit's
D XIIs is seen in this fine in-flight
photograph, displaying the *Staffel*
marking of a white chevron on
the upper wing. A black chevron
insignia was probably also carried
on the undersides of the lower
wings (*A Imrie*)

Ltn d R Rudolf Fuchs of *Jasta* 77b
shows off the Heinecke parachute
harness as he poses with his Pfalz
D XII (possibly 1346/18). This was
an early-production machine with
the first form of roughly rectangular
rudder. Apparently the cooling
system was not functioning very
well, as additional ventilation holes
have been cut into the nose, right
and left deflectors have been
mounted on the radiator and the
rear panel of the engine cowling
has been removed. An anemometer-
type ASI is affixed to the port inner
interplane strut

Another view of Rudolf Fuchs' D XII
of *Jasta* 77b. The early form of fin
and rudder is evident. The tail (and
apparently the nose) was painted
blue as a *Staffel* marking. The
fuselage cross bears evidence
of an earlier form that has been
overpainted. Fuchs served in both
Bavarian *Jagdstaffeln* 35 and 77, and
attained one victory with the latter
unit on 25 September 1918

'What is a Pfalz D XII? No one has ever heard of such a machine, and
no one knows anything about it. We decline to take these machines. The
result is a series of long telephone conversations. We are told that they are
very good, better than Fokkers in some regards (eyewash!), and we must
take them. There are no more Fokkers to be had, and in any case these
new Pfalz are better than the old Albatros, and when new Fokkers come
along we can take them in exchange. All right then, we'll have the Pfalz.

'Each of us climbed into the new machines with a prejudice against them
and immediately tried to find as many faults as possible. The *Staffel* opinion
was the same as ours. The *Werkmeister* grumbled because of the trouble the
rigging was going to make for him, while the mechanics cursed because of
the extra work to assemble and dismantle them, and declared them awkward
to handle. No one wanted to fly those Pfalz except under compulsion, and
those who had to made as much fuss as they could about practising on them.

'Later, the pilots got on very well with them. They flew quite decently
and could always keep pace with the Fokkers. Those who flew the Pfalz did
so because there were no other machines for them. But they always gazed
enviously at the Fokkers and prayed for the quick chance of an exchange.'

When interviewed by Peter M Grosz, Stark said;

'During larger operations we flew both the Fokker D VII and Pfalz
D XII in unison. Both types were similar, but the Fokker was more

maneouvrable. Therefore, I gave the Pfalz pilots instructions that during attacks by the enemy, they were to fly below the Fokkers.'

An especially harsh critic of the D XII was Joachim von Hippel, the technical officer of *Jasta* 71 at Habsheim in the *Armee Abteilung 'B'* sector. His diary recorded;

'12/9/18 – The *Jasta* was assigned new Pfalz D XII. These aircraft are extremely difficult to fly and the undercarriage usually breaks when landing. To sum up, my flight has absolutely no use for these crates whatsoever.

'16/9/18 – Flying Pfalz D XII 2675/18, I crashed and heavily damaged the aircraft on landing. Soon after this, Vfw Sieg crashed from a low altitude over the field and was immediately killed. As *Jagdstaffel* technical officer, I made and submitted the following report at once to the proper authorities;

'"The single seat fighter Pfalz D XII was assigned to *Jasta* 71 for combat evaluation and is herewith rejected for the following reasons;

'1) Despite the use of a high-compression engine, the aircraft climbs very poorly above 3000 metres.

An unidentified pilot of *Jasta* 77b strikes a confident pose with a Pfalz D XII thought to be 394/18. This was an early-production machine with the initial style of fin and rudder, and it also boasted the *Staffel* markings of a blue nose and tail. The black(?) swastika was a personal insignia, and at this time was known only as a common good luck totem, with no political significance. An anemometer has been affixed, and a rectangular foresight is also in place (*SHAA B89-4338*)

'2) When banking the aircraft into a turn, normal altitude cannot be maintained since the sluggishness in the controls in the turn causes the aeroplane to lose 150 metres. In combat against two French Breguets, the D XII lost excessive altitude and, when attempting to regain combat position in a climbing turn, the aircraft falls off. If the pilot is successful in correcting his flight attitude from a climbing turn the aircraft then shakes excessively, which can only be corrected by falling off in a slight dive.

'3) The take-off roll is extremely long, and landings with the D XII are very difficult and always almost end with the destruction of the machine."

'Bavarian *Staffeln* occupying the Habsheim airfield and flying the same aircraft have been observed, on a number of occasions, to crash their Pfalz D XII on landing through no fault of their own.

'3/10/18 – As a result of my test report, a pilot of the Pfalz Works flew the unpopular D XII in magnificent manoeuvres, but the Fokker D VII was still better. This was borne out in friendly combat between the Pfalz pilot in the D XII and myself in the D VII.'

As might be expected, a number of Bavarian *Jagdstaffeln* received the D XII, including *Staffeln* 23, 34, 35, 76, 77 and 78. *Jasta* 32b was also issued with a few D XIIs in late August. On 3 September *Jasta* 34b was

On 15 September 1918 SE 5as of No 1 Sqn and Bristol F 2B Fighters of No 62 Sqn forced Ltn d R Paul Vogel of *Jasta* 23b down behind British lines. Taken PoW, the Pfalz pilot later died of his wounds. The victory was shared by 2Lt D E Cameron of No 1 Sqn and Capt W E Staton and Lt L E Mitchell of No 62 Sqn . Vogel's Pfalz D XII 2486/18 came down quite intact, but the airframe was immediately set upon by souvenir-hungry British infantrymen, who, in ten minutes removed 'all the instruments, black crosses, magnetos and a large portion of the fabric and 3-ply'. This photograph, taken at No 2 Aeroplane Supply Depot, shows the damage that was done by the 'Tommies'. The Ministry of Munitions Report on this machine stated that 'The fabric is the usual colour-printed variety, and the body painted dark purple from nose to rear of the engine, bluish-grey to the pilot's cockpit and a dark green shading to a light pea-green extending to the tail. The fin and rudder are creamy-white, as is the part of the body above the tailplane, but the tailplanes themselves and the underneath portion of the body at the tail are painted in broad stripes of alternate black and white'. The black and white décor on the tail section formed the usual unit marking of *Jasta* 23b (*M O'Connor*)

A unique view of the starboard side of Ltn d R Vogel's D XII 2486/18 provides further details of the markings, although the fabric pieces ripped off the wreckage make it difficult to determine exactly what the aeroplane originally looked like. It would appear that the fuselage cross fabric was cut and torn off the plywood frame, and large sections of the unit marking were also removed. The report on this machine also commented on the gunnery of the No 1 Sqn pilots who attacked the D XII. 'Our pilots made some excellent shooting during the combat, there being a group of shots about 12 inches in diameter through the 3-ply at the back of the pilot's seat, and a similar group on the starboard side of the fuselage about 18 inches behind the pilot's seat' (*M O'Connor*)

forced to retreat to Bevillers, where it was supplied with new D XIIs. The *Jasta* war diary reported that the D XIIs were inferior to contemporary British fighters, and this had a demoralising effect on those pilots issued with the Pfalz.

Allied intelligence reports based on prisoner interrogations echoed these sentiments. One bulletin that was issued in September 1918 reads, 'Speed and climb of the D XII are better than the Fokker D VII, but it is unpopular owing to indifferent manoeuvrability and it is also difficult to land.'

Other units that were allocated D XIIs included *Jagdstaffeln* 3, 17, 36, 37, 43, 49, 61, 64w, 65, 71, 73 and 81. *Jasta* 36, desperate for replacement machines, travelled to AFP 17 to pick up eight D XIIs on 4 October 1918. Its pilots found the fighters' engine plugs had been thoroughly fouled by 'used oil', and they also had worn rings – remedying these problems took precious time. On 8 November the *Jasta* retreated to Lierme, and because of poor weather the Pfalz could not be flown out and so were all burned.

In conclusion, the Pfalz D XII was a more than adequate replacement for obsolescent Albatros and Pfalz D IIIa fighters (about 470 of these were still at the front at the end of August). When well maintained and flown by a skilled pilot, the D XII could perform quite well. However, it had the bad luck to arrive after the Fokker D VII, and inevitably suffered in comparison. Had there been enough of the superb BMW D IIIa engines to equip D XIIs in quantity, it might have been a different story.

APPENDICES

COLOUR PLATES

Artist Harry Dempsey worked tirelessly with the author to illustrate the aeroplanes featured in the colour section as accurately as circumstances will permit. Some of the illustrations are based on limited evidence and are noted as provisional, and the colours portrayed are generally approximations only. The research and assistance of Alex Imrie and Manfred Thiemeyer is gratefully acknowledged, and the work of Dan-San Abbott, Colin Owers and Ray Rimell was also of great use.

1
Pfalz Parasol P39 of Vfw Otto Kissenberth, *Feldflieger Abteilung* 9b, Toblach, June 1915
Kissenberth's Parasol is shown in the red and white markings applied for the Cortina raid of 3 June 1915. Otherwise, the aircraft was covered in clear-doped fabric of a light yellowish or cream appearance, with white fields for the numerous iron cross applications. The Parasols and later E-types had the borders of their fuselages, wings and control surfaces marked in black, most likely with dyed tapes. Metal cowlings, nose panels and struts were treated with black enamel, and the serial P39 was applied in several locations. The makeshift wooden bomb container for five 4.5-kg Carbonit-Bombs is shown on the fuselage side.

2
Pfalz E I 215/15 of Offz Stv Willy Rosenstein, *Feldflieger Abteilung* 19, Porcher, December 1915
All of the Pfalz E-types were covered in a bleached fabric, which presented a very white appearance. All metal cowlings, nose panels and undercarriages were black. This E I was unusual in that the serial number was applied (almost certainly at the unit level) in large ornate characters.

3
Pfalz D III 1396/17 of Oblt Oskar Freiherr von Boenigk, *Jasta* 4, Marckebeeke, circa October 1917
This machine shows the black spiral band that comprised the unit marking of *Jasta* 4. Pilots' individual markings generally took the form of coloured tail sections and occasionally spinners. A photograph of this aircraft seems to show that the uppersurface of the lower wing was painted a dark, glossy colour that the author has *tentatively* identified as the yellow associated with von Boenigk's old grenadier regiment. It now seems likely that the entire length of the wing was so treated. The tail and spinner of this machine are provisionally shown as yellow.

4
Pfalz D III (serial unknown) of Ltn d R Werner Voss, *Jasta* 10, Marcke, September 1917
It is emphasised that this is also a tentative illustration, based on one poor photo that Heinz Nowarra captioned as Voss'

D III. Two black bands on either side of the fuselage cross can be seen in the photo, as well as the early less extensive form of yellow *Jasta* colouration on the nose. The similarity of the two black stripes to those seen on the familiar photographs of Vfw Hecht's D III D.1370/17 has led to speculation that Voss' D III was the same aircraft in an earlier guise. *Perhaps* the aircraft was taken over by Hecht after Voss' death, and the green tail and further yellow colouration was added.

5
Pfalz D III 1395/17 of Ltn d R Aloys Heldmann, *Jasta* 10, Marcke, September 1917
A few of the aircraft in the first production batch of the D III were terrain camouflaged on the uppersurfaces like the Roland D III machines the factory had been building. This two-tone colour scheme probably consisted of shades of purple and green as illustrated, although reddish-brown may have been used instead of purple. The undersides were a light colour, probably *silbergrau* or pale blue. The photograph of Heldmann seated on the wheel of this machine shows a very light coloured wheel cover which is here interpreted as blue – a colour favoured by Heldmann for personal identification. At some point the yellow *Jasta* markings may have been added as well.

6
Pfalz D III (serial unknown) of Ltn d R Hans Klein, *Jasta* 10, Marcke, circa November 1917
Klein appeared in at least two photos with this D III, and it is assumed to have been one of his own machines. Previously, the lengthwise fuselage band has been depicted as *Jasta* 10 yellow, but a recently acquired photo shows that it was more likely black, and extended on to the *Staffel* marking on the nose. The yellow colouration of the tail is also assumed.

7
Pfalz D IIIa 4117/17 of Ltn d R Aloys Heldmann, *Jasta* 10, Marcke, November 1917
This illustration is based on excerpts from Heldmann's combat reports compiled by historian W Puglisi and on file at the History of Aviation Collection, UTD. These indicate that Heldmann's third victory on 29 November 1917 was scored in 4117/17, and that the aircraft had a blue tail. The shade of blue depicted is entirely arbitrary, and the standard *Jasta* markings are shown.

8
Pfalz D III 4059/17 of Ltn d R Heinrich Arntzen, *Jasta* 15, Le Clos Ferme, December 1917
At this time the aircraft of *Jasta* 15 displayed individual markings only. Arntzen, a former observer with considerable experience as a photographer, chose to use the Prussian

Observer's Badge as his personal emblem. This consisted of the black/white Hohenzollern crest within a red border.

9
Pfalz D III 1416/17 of Ltn d R Hans Müller, *Jasta* 15, Le Clos Ferme, November 1917
Hans Müller applied his usual emblem of a fuselage band of diagonal black(?) and white stripes to his D III – the location is assumed to be Le Clos Ferme. These black/white stripes were also applied to his earlier OAW-built Albatros D III and to his later Fokker Dr I. The latter also displayed stripes in chevron form on the tailplane/elevators, and a close inspection of the photograph shows that the tail of this Pfalz was similarly decorated.

10
Pfalz D IIIa (serial unknown) of Hptm Rudolf Berthold, *Jagdgeschwader* II, Balatre, April 1918
The extent of combat use of this familiar D IIIa by the semi-crippled *Kommandeur* remains debatable. It displayed the familiar 'Berthold colours' of a red nose with dark blue fuselage and wing uppersurfaces, along with the celebrated winged sword emblem. The underside of the fuselage is shown as untouched silver-grey – a feature that was universal on the other Pfalz in *Jasta* 15/18 (the Albatros similarly featured light blue undersides). The undersides of the wings and tailplane were also *silbergrau*.

11
Pfalz D IIIa (serial unknown) on Ltn d R Hans Müller, *Jasta* 18, Fachez by Lille, April 1918
After Müller and his comrades were transferred to *Jasta* 18, he went on to fly this D IIIa in the flamboyant *Staffel* 'Raben' red and white colours. The upper wing surfaces were vermilion red along with the nose, which featured a white spinner. A photograph of this aircraft shows the famous black raven emblem in effect, but does not reveal whether or not any fuselage cross was applied – it has not been illustrated, but remains plausible. Much of the aft fuselage is speculative, as are the date and location data.

12
Pfalz D IIIa (serial unknown) of Ltn d R Carl Degelow, *Jasta* 7, Roulers, late March(?) 1918
This profile is based on the well-known photo of Degelow's overturned Pfalz. The details and date of this photo are not recorded, and the condition of the D IIIa in the image obscures many details. It may be that this photo depicts an event on 23 March 1918, when Jacobs' diary states that Degelow turned his aircraft over whilst landing. In the photo, a piece of the mangled tail section is visible painted black and white – this has led the author to assume that the rudder had been partially painted white during the conversion to the new *Balkenkreuz* insignia. If the date of 23 March is accurate then the *Jasta* 7 crewmen were quick to repaint the insignia, as the order for the new format was only issued on 17 March. The wings and all struts seem to have been painted black as well.

13
Pfalz D III 4011/17 of Ltn d R Fritz Höhn, *Jasta* 21s, Villers la Chèvre, circa December 1917

The black and white unit marking was intersected by Höhn's zigzag red stripes on his D III. The combination of various coloured stripes was thought to break up the outline of the aircraft and make it difficult for enemy ground gunners to hit. Höhn was beginning to specialise in attacks on kite balloons at this time. The additional personal number '10' beneath the serial number was also part of the *Staffel* livery.

14
Pfalz D IIIa 8009/17 of Ltn d R Fritz Höhn, *Jasta* 21s, St Mard, March 1918
Once again Höhn marked his D IIIa with zigzag red bands intended to confuse enemy gunners. His teddy bear mascot was often braced to the fuselage just behind the cockpit.

15
Pfalz D IIIa (serial unknown) of Ltn Busso von Alvensleben, Rocourt, June 1918
Although not an ace, von Alvensleben had flown with many celebrated airmen in *Jasta* 4 of JG I, and then in Saxon *Jasta* 21. He did attain a single victory on 14 June 1918 when he flamed a French balloon, only to be wounded and taken prisoner and die of his wounds on the 15th. Von Alvensleben's D IIIa displayed a spectacular overall colour scheme provisionally interpreted as black and white on all uppersurfaces, in conjunction with the unit markings. The uppersurfaces of all wings were painted in dark/light segments. The style of cross application is quite unique – the crosses shown on the wings are provisional, and the undersides of the wings retained their factory finish. There may have been some white serial number stencilling on the aft fuselage, but the photograph of this aircraft does not permit clarification. The circular Pfalz logo decal seen on the planform pages is a new and accurate rendition based on information from historian and collector Charles Gosse. This logo is often seen on the struts and wheel covers of Pfalz aircraft from the D III through to the D XII.

16
Pfalz D IIIa 5855/17 of Ltn d R Josef Schäfer, *Jasta* 16b, Le Cateau, circa March 1918
Schäfer was another non-ace, but he did obtain three confirmed victories. His D IIIa displayed the typical black tail unit marking of Bavarian *Jasta* 16, along with some flamboyant black stripes as personal insignia. Most Pfalz of this *Staffel* also seem to have boasted black spinners.

17
Pfalz D IIIa (serial unknown) of Oblt d R Fritz Röth, *Jasta* 16b, Ste Marguerite, circa May 1918
Readers are again cautioned that this is a provisional illustration based on a photo of dubious provenance. The image is thought to show *Staffelführer* Röth in a Pfalz D IIIa of *Jasta* 16b, but it does not reveal the tail of the aircraft. The pilot's personal insignia was the black(?) and white fuselage sash. It is unknown if the port side of the fuselage featured a mirror image of this sash, or whether it continued down at a rearward angle to terminate at the aft fuselage. The absence of a fuselage cross is also puzzling. The author expresses his thanks to Dan-San Abbott for information about this aircraft.

18
Pfalz D III 1405/17 of Vfw Jakob Landin, *Jasta* 32b, Autremencourt, December 1917

Landin's Pfalz featured a stylish rendition of the unit's black tail and black/white nose markings. Landin's 'L' initial was applied as a personal emblem, along with black wheel discs. Landin achieved three victories. He was flying Pfalz D IIIa 5897/17 on 27 February 1918 when he crashed upon returning to Guesnain airfield 30 minutes after take-off. Both the aircraft and its pilot were consumed by the ensuing fire.

19
Pfalz D III 4064/17 of Ltn d R Rudolf Stark, *Jasta* 34b, Chenois by Virton, February 1918

This was apparently Stark's first Pfalz, flown after his arrival at Bavarian *Jasta* 34. The *Staffel* marking was a silver or 'silvery-white' fuselage, applied to the unit's Albatros fighters using stocks of Pfalz factory *silbergrau* paint which had been supplied to the unit when its D IIIs were acquired. The unit's Pfalz fighters thus already had this *Staffel* 'marking', and Stark's personal emblems of a lilac fuselage band and spinner were the only special markings applied.

20
Pfalz D IIIa 8155/17 of Ltn d R Rudolf Stark, *Jasta* 34b, Foucaucourt, April 1918

Stark flew several different D IIIa fighters during his time in *Jasta* 34b, and this one displayed an early thick form of *Balkenkreuz* insignia with complete white borders. The rudder was painted white, and the aircraft again boasted Stark's lilac band and spinner. Thanks to Dan-San Abbott for information on this D IIIa.

21
Pfalz D IIIa 8170/17 of Ltn d R Hans Böhning, *Jasta* 79b, Villeselve, May 1918

A number of aircraft in the final two batches of D IIIa machines were covered in five-colour printed camouflage fabric on the wings and control surfaces, and D IIIa 8170/17 was one of these. The fuselage was painted an extremely dark colour, which does not comply with the usual light shade of 'Bavarian blue'. It is therefore theorised that the *Jasta* used black as a unit marking, just as Bavarian *Staffeln* 16, 23 and 32 did for a period. Böhning had his initials 'HB' applied as a personal emblem, and it is noteworthy that this insignia also resembles the logo of the famous *Hofbräuhaus* brewery in Munich! The aft fuselage depiction is entirely provisional, as it is not seen in the only available photo. The author's gratitude is extended to Manfred Thiemeyer for helpful information.

22
Pfalz D III 1386/17 of Ltn d R Alfred Lenz, *Jasta* 22, Mont, September 1917

Lenz was the *Staffelführer* of this *Jasta*, and he decorated his machine with black personal markings on the fuselage. The planform view shows the additional markings on the tailplane and wings. Lenz survived the war with six confirmed claims.

23
Pfalz D III 5983/17 of Oblt Hans Joachim Buddecke, *Jasta* 30, Phalempin, February 1918

The famous 'Blue Max' ace Buddecke served only briefly in *Jasta* 30, but was photographed with this D IIIa. It seems possible that the well known orange diamond insignia of this *Staffel* was not yet in effect, or that Buddecke was allowed to exercise more personal choice in the decoration of his machine. It was marked with what is thought to be a stylised black heart emblem around the fuselage cross.

24
Pfalz D IIIa 4203/17 of Ltn Hans-Georg von der Marwitz, *Jasta* 30, Phalempin, March 1918

The unique black-bordered orange diamond unit marking of *Jagdstaffel* 30 is in full display on D IIIa 4203/17. It was generally applied to the fuselage sides, the centre section of the upper wing and in various formats to the tailplane and elevator. Von der Marwitz personalised his aircraft by extending the unit colour to the entire tail section, even obliterating the national insignia on the rudder.

25
Pfalz D IIIa 8233/17 of Oblt Hans Bethge, *Jasta* 30, Phalempin, March 1918

Although the only photographs of this machine show it with *Balkenkreuz* markings while flown by Ltn Kaus, it seems likely that this aircraft was previously flown by Oblt Bethge before his death in a different D IIIa on 17 March 1918. As such it is depicted with iron cross insignia. A reference in Otto Fuchs' fictionalised account of his time in *Jasta* 30 (*Wir Flieger*) describes the *Staffelführer* as flying a machine striped in grey and white – thus this provisional attribution. The wings were covered in five-colour fabric, and the fuselage was entirely striped in grey and white. Again the author's debt to Manfred Thiemeyer for information is acknowledged, and the research of Bruno Schmäling is also noted.

26
Pfalz D IIIa (serial unknown) of Ltn Hans-Georg von der Marwitz, *Jasta* 30, Phalempin, May 1918

This D IIIa appears in the background of the photo of von der Marwitz with his captured opponent Lt W E Cowan of No 208 Sqn, brought down on 16 May. The entire fuselage and the uppersurfaces of both wings appear to have been painted a dark colour. Several references in Fuchs' *Wir Flieger* and data from Alex Imrie and Manfred Thiemeyer all indicate that this Pfalz of von der Marwitz was a wine-red or dark burgundy, a striking colour scheme for the aircraft of the *Staffelführer*. Again, the fuselage cross was obliterated as part of the individual colour display. The markings on the tail section are entirely provisional.

27
Pfalz D IIIa of Uffz Werner Hertel, *Jasta* 40s, Lomme, circa June 1918

Although he was no ace, Werner Hertel certainly flew alongside such *Jasta* 40 notables as Degelow and Rosenstein. His D IIIa boasted the *Staffel* colour scheme of a white tail with black fuselage, struts and undercarriage, as well as his striking personal badge of a detailed winged dagger. The wings were seemingly covered in five-colour fabric, and bore full-chord late style *Balkenkreuz* insignia. While no photos are known of Degelow's *Jasta* 40s Pfalz, his machine would likely have been very similar, except for his usual white stag emblem. A junior pilot of the *Jasta*, Hertel continued to fly his Pfalz after most of the other pilots had D VIIs, although he eventually received his own Fokker too.

28
Pfalz D IIIa 4229/17 of Vfw Carl Bücker, *Kest* 8w, Varsenaere, circa February 1918

Photos of *Kest* 8w Albatros and Pfalz fighters reveal that they were marked with a serpent coiled around the fuselage, although the precise colour and number of 'coils' of the snake emblem varied from one machine to another. The serpent painted on 4229/17 is provisionally shown as a very dark green. This Pfalz does not seem to display the light-coloured tail section seen on other machines of the unit, although the fuselage and rudder cross were both outlined in white. Each *Kest* 8w machine also bore a small white individual number on the nose, in this case a '3' above the lower wing root.

29
Pfalz D VIII 124/18(?) of Ltn d R Paul Bäumer, *Jasta* 'Boelcke', Vivaise, May 1918

The fuselage of Bäumer's D VIII is shown as the familiar *silbergrau* seen on earlier types, but it is possible a more flat shade of bluish-grey was applied to D VIIIs and D XIIs. The wings were covered in five-colour 'lozenge' fabric, and the *Jasta* 'Boelcke' black/white unit markings were painted onto the tail and engine cowling. Bäumer's personal insignia of a red/white/black chevron was applied to the fuselage.

30
Pfalz D VIII 178/18 of Ltn d R Ludwig Beckmann, *Jasta* 56, Rumbeke Ost, circa May 1918

The aircraft of *Jasta* 56 first featured yellow noses and tails, but in later years Beckmann recalled that his own Fokker D VII was marked with those components in red. Thus his Pfalz has been provisionally illustrated here with a red nose and tail, although yellow is just as likely. The cross style shown on the fuselage is also tentative, and this D VIII probably served long enough with the *Jasta* to feature the later style of *Balkenkreuz* as well.

31
Pfalz D XII 1346/18 of Ltn d R Rudolf Fuchs, *Jasta* 77b, St Marie, Vouziers, circa August 1918

Fuchs' D XII was an early production machine with the initial form of 'rectangular' fin and rudder, which displayed the unit's blue tail marking. Part of the nose was also blue, and the fuselage cross was converted from an earlier style with neutral paint. The wings were covered in five-colour fabric. Rudolf Fuchs downed a SPAD at Arnaville on 25 September for his sole confirmed victory.

32
Pfalz D XII 2525/18 of Vfw Ludwig Marchner, *Jasta* 32b, Lieu St Amand, circa September 1918

By late 1918 *Jasta* 32b had abandoned its former unit marking of a black tail in favour of 'Bavarian blue' markings, which in this case take the form of the pilot's initial applied to the fuselage immediately below the cockpit. The sequence of camouflage colours illustrated is one of several variations, and is a very provisional choice based on colours recorded in a report on 2685/18 – the nose purple, then medium grey, dark green, light green, purple, then medium grey and dark green again. Marchner chalked up two victories, the last one recorded on 30 October 1918.

BIBLIOGRAPHY

Bock, Dr G, 'The History of Bavarian *Jagdstaffel* 16', *Cross & Cockade Journal,* Vol 8 No 4, 1967

Bock, Dr G, 'The Royal Bavarian *Jagdstaffel* 34', *Cross & Cockade Journal,* Vol 16 No 4, 1975

Bodenschatz, K, *Jagd in Flanderns Himmel,* Munich, 1935

Duiven, R (ed), Cooper, M, '*Jagdstaffel 47w* – A History', *Over the Front,* Vol 10 No 4, 1995

Flanagan, Dr B P, 'The Holtzem Story', *Cross & Cockade Journal,* Vol 12 No 2, 1971

Franks, N, Bailey, F and Duiven, R, *The Jasta Pilots,* London, 1996

Franks, N, Bailey, F and Duiven, R, *The Jasta War Chronology,* London, 1998

Franks, N, Bailey, F, and Guest, R, *Above the Lines,* London, 1993

Gill, R, 'The Albums of Willy Rosenstein', *Cross & Cockade Journal,* Vol 25 No 4, 1984

Gray, P L, *Profile Publications 43 – Pfalz D III,* Leatherhead, Surrey, 1965

Grosz, P M and Krüger, E, *Pfalz – First Detailed Story of the Company and its Famous Planes,* West Roxbury, 1964

Grosz, P M, *Pfalz D III Windsock Datafile 107,* Berkhamsted, 2004

Grosz, P M, *Pfalz D IIIa Windsock Datafile 21,* Berkhamsted, 1990

Grosz, P M, *Pfalz D XII Windsock Datafile 41,* Berkhamsted, 1993

Grosz, P M, *Pfalz E I – E VI Windsock Datafile 59,* Berkhamsted, 1996

Herris, J, *Pfalz Aircraft of World War 1,* Boulder, CO, 2001

Imrie, A, *Osprey Airwar 17 – German Fighter Units June 1917-1918,* London, 1978

Imrie, A, *Vintage Warbirds 16 – German Army Air Aces of World War One,* Poole, 1987

Jentsch, K F Kurt, *Jagdflieger im Feuer,* Magdeburg, 1937

Jones, I, *An Air Fighter's Scrapbook,* London, 1938

Jones, I, *King of Air Fighters,* London, 1934

Jones, I, *Tiger Squadron,* London, 1954

Kastner, R, *Bayerische Flieger im Hochgebirge,* Gröbenzell, 1998

Lawson, S T (ed), '*Jasta 7* Under "Kobes"', *Cross & Cockade International Journal,* Vol 25 Nos 2 and 3, 1984

Lawson, S T, 'Royal Prussian *Jagdstaffel* Nr 30', *Cross & Cockade International Journal,* Vol 31 No 2, 2000

Lambrecht, E, *Versteende vleugels,* Kortrijk, 2005

Mückler, J, *Aus der Chronik der Jagdstaffel 32,* Zweibrücken, 2001

O'Connor, N, *Aviation Awards of Imperial Germany in World War 1 and the Men Who Earned Them,* Vols I to VII, Princeton NJ and Atglen PA, 1988 to 2003

Puglisi, W, (ed), 'Raesch of *Jasta* 43', *Cross & Cockade Journal,* Vol 8 No 4, 1967

Schmäling, B, 'One of those Flyers – Vfw Ludwig Walk, Royal Bavarian *Jasta* 79b and 77b', *Cross & Cockade Great Britain Journal,* Vol 11 No 1, 1980

Stark, R, *Die Jagdstaffel unsere Heimat,* Leipzig, 1932

Zuerl, W, *Pour le Mérite-Flieger,* Munich, 1938

ACKNOWLEDGEMENTS

The author owes a great debt to many people for their help in compiling this work. Peter M Grosz started it all with the gracious loan of his photographs and his indispensable research and example. Alex Imrie also provided valuable photographs and advice based on his pioneering research. Manfred Thiemeyer generously provided rare photographs and insights too. The staff of the History of Aviation Collection at the *University of Texas* at Dallas were, as always, extremely helpful. O'Brien Browne kindly translated significant German texts. Stephen Lawson graciously gave of his vast knowledge of Josef Jacobs. Chip Minx generously shared his rare photographs from the Hertel album and Eddy Lambrecht provided rare MFJ photographs. Thanks are extended to Terry 'Taz' Phillips and to the research staff at the USAF Museum who went to such effort to provide copies of the Arthur Rahn albums. Dan-San Abbott, Lance Bronnenkant, Jörn Leckscheid, George H Williams, Jack Herris, Aaron Weaver, Ray Rimell, Dr Dieter H M Gröschel, Norman Franks, Reinhard Kastner and too many others to name all gave unselfishly of their time and material. Rick Duiven's assistance and *Jasta* listings were extremely valuable as always. The author's many colleagues at *Over the Front* (www.overthefront.com), *Cross and Cockade International* (www.crossandcockade.com) and the Aerodrome Forum (www.theaerodrome.com) were helpful as usual, and their publications are highly recommended.

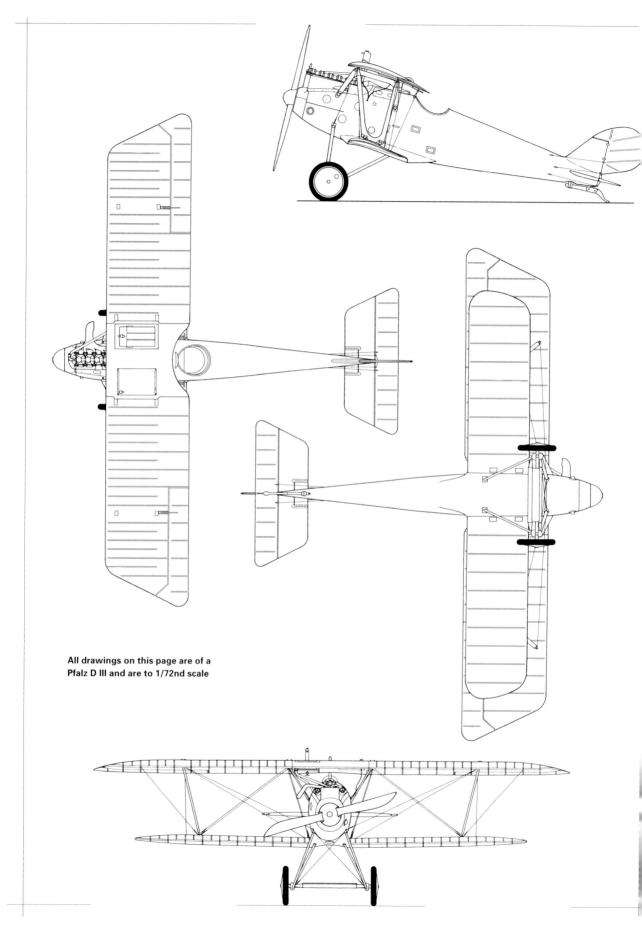

All drawings on this page are of a
Pfalz D III and are to 1/72nd scale

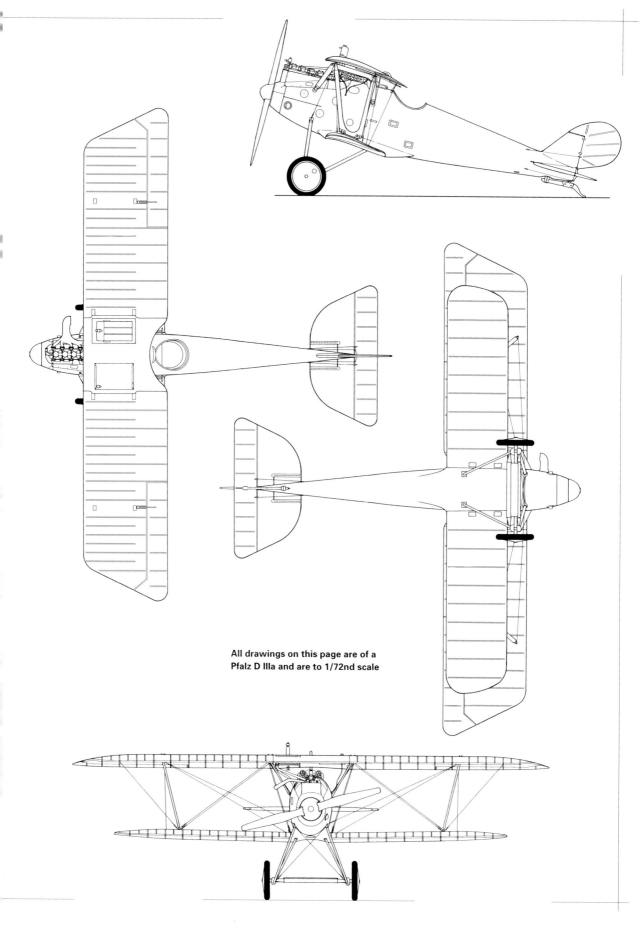

All drawings on this page are of a
Pfalz D IIIa and are to 1/72nd scale

INDEX